IMAGES OF WAR

US Naval Aviation
1945–2003

An F-4J Phantom II landing aboard the USS *Constellation* (CVA-64) in 1974. *NMNA*

IMAGES OF WAR

US Naval Aviation 1945–2003

RARE PHOTOGRAPHS FROM NAVAL ARCHIVES

LEO MARRIOTT

Pen & Sword
AVIATION
AN IMPRINT OF PEN & SWORD BOOKS LTD.
YORKSHIRE – PHILADELPHIA

First published in Great Britain in 2023 by
PEN & SWORD AVIATION
An imprint of
Pen & Sword Books Ltd
Yorkshire – Philadelphia

ISBN 978 1 39906 257 2

Typeset in 12/14.5 Gill Sans by SJmagic DESIGN SERVICES, India.

Printed and bound in England by CPI Group (UK) Ltd, Croydon, CR0 4YY.

Pen & Sword Books Ltd incorporates the imprints of Pen & Sword Archaeology, Atlas, Aviation, Battleground, Discovery, Family History, History, Maritime, Military, Naval, Politics, Social History, Transport, True Crime, Claymore Press, Frontline Books, Praetorian Press, Seaforth Publishing and White Owl.

For a complete list of Pen & Sword titles please contact:

PEN & SWORD BOOKS LTD
George House, Units 12 & 13, Beevor Street, Off Pontefract Road, Barnsley, South Yorkshire, S71 1HN, England
E-mail: enquiries@pen-and-sword.co.uk
Website: www.pen-and-sword.co.uk

or

PEN AND SWORD BOOKS
1950 Lawrence Rd, Havertown, PA 19083, USA
E-mail: Uspen-and-sword@casematepublishers.com
Website: www.penandswordbooks.com

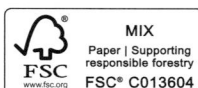

MIX
Paper | Supporting
responsible forestry
FSC
www.fsc.org   FSC® C013604

Contents

Glossary and Abbreviations   7

Introduction   11

Chapter 1:   The Post-War Legacy, 1945–1950   13

Chapter 2:   The Korean War, 1950–1953   32

Chapter 3:   Supersonics and Supercarriers, 1954–1965   51

Chapter 4:   The Vietnam Era, 1965–1975   73

Chapter 5:   Helicopters and ASW   92

Chapter 6:   AEW and Electronic Warfare   112

Chapter 7:   Taming the Bear, 1975–1990   125

Chapter 8:   Hot Action after the Cold War, 1990–2003   140

Chapter 9:   Supporting the Front Line   156

Chapter 10:   Pushing the Boundaries   167

Photo Credits   177

Bibliography   178

Glossary and Abbreviations

AA	Anti-Aircraft
AEW	Airborne Early Warning
AFB	Air Force Base
ASUW	Anti-Surface Warfare
ASW	Anti-Submarine Warfare
ATG	Air Task Group
C-in-C	Commander-in-Chief
CAG or CVG	Carrier Air Group
CAP	Combat Air Patrol
COD	Carrier On-Board Delivery
CVW	Carrier Air Wing
DP	Dual-Purpose gun
ECCM	Electronic Counter Countermeasures
ECM	Electronic Countermeasures
ECMO	Electronic Countermeasures Operator
ELINT	Electronic Intelligence
ESM	Electronic Surveillance Measures
EW	Electronic Warfare
FIA	Fédération Aéronautique Internationale
FLIR	Forward-Looking Infra-Red
HARM	High-speed Anti-Radiation Missile
HMAS	Her Majesty's Australian Ship
HMS	His Majesty's Ship / Her Majesty's Ship
HVAR	High Velocity Aerial Rocket
ISR	Intelligence, Surveillance, Reconnaissance
JATO	Jet-Assisted Take-Off (actually using rockets)
j.g.	junior grade
KIA/MIA	Killed/Missing in Action
LAMPS	Light Airborne Multi-Purpose System
MAD	Magnetic Anomaly Detector

MAUW	Maximum All-Up Weight
NACA	National Advisory Committee for Aeronautics
NAS	Naval Air Station
NATC	Naval Air Test Centre
NATO	North Atlantic Treaty Organisation
NVAS	North Vietnamese Army
PR	Photographic Reconnaissance
RAF	Royal Air Force
RAN	Royal Australian Navy
RAS	Replenishment at Sea
RCVW	Readiness Carrier Air Wing
RN	Royal Navy
SAC	Strategic Air Command
SAR	Search and Rescue
SCB	Ship Characteristics Board
TF/TG	Task Force / Task Group
UN	United Nations
US	United States
USAAF	United States Army Air Forces
USAF	United States Air Force
USMC	United States Marine Corps
USS	United States Ship
VA	US Navy Attack Squadron
VB	US Navy Dive-Bomber Squadron
VF	US Navy Fighter Squadron
VFN	US Navy Night Fighter Squadron
VT	US Navy Torpedo Bomber Squadron
VX	US Navy Experimental Squadron

US Navy ship designations: US Navy ships were (and still are) identified by a combination of letters indicating the ship's role followed by a sequential number for that type of ship. The first US aircraft carrier (USS *Langley*) was designated CV-1, the letters CV standing for Carrier – Heavier than Air (to distinguish it from ships designed to support airship operations) and subsequent carriers received sequential numbers. Designations for other classes of aircraft carrier included CVL (Light Aircraft Carrier) and CVE (Escort Carrier). After the Second World War, the prefix was changed in some cases to reflect more specialised roles including CVS (anti-submarine carrier) and CVA (attack carrier), while the suffix N was added to indicate a nuclear-powered carrier. After 1975, all carriers reverted to CV or CVN as the specialised designations were no longer appropriate.

US Navy aircraft designations: Between 1922 and 1962, the US Navy adopted a standard system to identify each type and variant of its aircraft. This took the form of a letter or letters indicating the aircraft's function (e.g. F for Fighter), a sequential number for each design produced by a single company, and a letter to indicate the manufacturer. For example, the Vought Corsair was designated F4U, which indicated that it was the fourth fighter design (F4) produced by the Vought Division of the United Aircraft Corporation (U). In the case of the first design of that type by a company, the sequential number was omitted, the most obvious example being the Douglas Skyraider, which would have been the A1D, but was simply designated AD. A suffix number indicated the mark or variant (e.g. F4U-1, F4U-4) while an X prefix was applied to prototypes (e.g. XF4U-1). Finally, an additional letter was applied to indicate a variant modified for a specific role such as F4U-4N, which was a night fighter version of the standard F4U-1 Corsair.

In 1962, this system was changed in order to standardise aircraft designations throughout the US armed services. This was based on the USAF system which consisted of a function letter (or letters) with a number allocated in sequence to each new design as it appeared (e.g. F-86 Sabre, B-52 Stratofortress) but no prominent indication of the manufacturer. Many US Navy aircraft were redesignated simply by dropping the manufacturer's letter so that, for example, the A4D Skyhawk became the A-4 while the F8U Crusader became the F-8. However, where that would result in duplication with another aircraft type, a new number was allocated (e.g. the F4D Skyray became the F-6 to avoid confusion with the F4H Phantom II, which became the F-4). Subsequent variants were identified by a suffix letter (e.g. A-4E, F-4B). In cases where a USAF equivalent type already existed then that designation was adopted (e.g. Lockheed WV-2 Warning Star became the EC-121). After 1962, new aircraft types were given the next available sequential number in that category (e.g Grumman F-14 Tomcat).

US Navy and Marine Corps squadron designations: Squadrons are designated by a number prefixed by the letter V (or H for helicopter squadrons) and other letters defining the squadron's operational role (e.g. VF-32 – Navy Fighter Squadron 32). In the case of Marine squadrons, the letter M is inserted immediately following the V (e.g. VMF-451). Most squadrons adopted a nickname that in many cases was officially approved, while, over time, the same name may have been used by several different squadrons. In this book, where appropriate, the nickname is given in parentheses after the squadron designation (e.g. VF-102 'Diamondbacks'). Tracing squadron histories and nicknames is difficult as they were often redesignated and sometimes the name and traditions of the previous squadron were adopted (e.g. in 1958, VF-123 'Blue

Racers' became VF-53 'Blue Knights'. Disestablished in 1962, a new squadron was formed in 1963 as VF-53 'Iron Angels'). The following is a list of the main squadron types referred to in this book:

VA	Attack	VAH	Heavy Attack
VAW	Airborne Early Warning	VC	Composite
VF	Fighter	VFA	Fighter Attack / Strike Fighter
VP	Patrol	VQ	Electronic Warfare
VS	Anti-submarine	VT	Training
HS	Helicopter ASW	HU	Helicopter Utility

Introduction

This book describes the development of US naval aviation after the end of the Second World War in August 1945 and is a companion volume to an earlier book in the Images of War series, which covered the period 1898 to 1945. In 1945, the US Navy was the largest in the world by any standard and in particular was able to deploy substantial numbers of aircraft carriers. In terms of numbers, it completely overshadowed Britain's Royal Navy, which had played a supportive role in the closing stages of the war against Japan. Inevitably, with the end of hostilities, the size of the active navy and aircraft carrier fleet was drastically reduced, not only because they were no longer needed to be in action, but also because with the defeat of the Axis powers there was no credible threat to the power of the US Navy (at that time the Soviet Navy was virtually non-existent in terms of operational capability).

In the remaining decades of the twentieth century, US naval aviation responded to a series of different challenges including technical advances, political infighting, and financial constraints as well as actual combat and warfare. The solutions to these issues were shown by the changes in ships, aircraft, tactics and force composition described in this book. In terms of numbers of ships and aircraft, Naval Aviation was considerably smaller in 2003 than it was in 1945, but in terms of capability and striking power, it has advanced out of all recognition. Major changes include the introduction of jet aircraft and helicopters while the nuclear-powered supercarriers provided a hitherto unattainable degree of operational flexibility.

This book traces the progress of these changes starting with the post-war uncertainties of the late 1940s and the introduction of jet aircraft. This was followed by the unexpected Korean War, which vindicated the role of the Navy's carriers and led to the construction of larger carriers and a new breed of supersonic combat aircraft. No sooner had these changes been absorbed than the Navy became heavily involved in the Vietnam War and painful new lessons had to be learnt. After the withdrawal from Vietnam, the US Navy had to face the growing strength of the Soviet Navy, but at least the Reagan administration of the 1980s provided the backing for an increase in the strength and capability of the fleet and its carriers. Ultimately, this

The Grumman F9F-6 was the US Navy's first swept-wing jet fighter. This example was flown by VF-61 'Jolly Rogers' aboard the USS *Intrepid* (CVA-11) in 1956. *NARA*

was instrumental in the end of the so-called Cold War but paradoxically opened the way to other conflicts, notably in the Balkans and then in the Middle East, Afghanistan and the Gulf Wars. All of these events and changes are recorded in this book with contemporary images covering the period from the end of the Second World War in 1945 to the end of the initial invasion of Iraq and the toppling of Saddam Hussein in 2003.

Chapter 1

The Post-War Legacy
1945-1950

At the beginning of September 1945, US naval aviation was at the peak of its strength in preparation for the final invasion of Japan, and in total the Navy possessed twenty-nine fast fleet carriers and sixty-nine small escort carriers, as well as 41,272 aircraft of all types. With the end of hostilities there was an inevitable and immediate reduction in these numbers and orders for new aircraft were either cut back or cancelled while orders for many ships were cancelled, including some already under construction. Many of the aircraft carriers, notably the large Essex class, were employed as troopships in Operation Magic Carpet, in which thousands of service personnel deployed overseas were brought home to be discharged.

However, technical advances were about to change the face of naval aviation and render many of its front-line aircraft obsolete overnight. The most significant factor was that the nature of war had potentially changed with the advent of the atomic bomb, which had brought about the capitulation of Japan. In the new atomic era, the viability of conventional carrier forces was seriously questioned, particularly by the newly formed and independent United States Air Force (previously administered by the Army as the US Army Air Force). A major political battle broke out between the Navy and the Air Force, the former wishing to build new aircraft carriers operating nuclear-armed bombers while the latter proposed a fleet of the new Convair B-36 inter-continental bombers. At the time the decision went in favour of the Air Force, which was a severe blow to the Navy's aspirations and forced the cancellation of the 68,000-ton USS *United Sates*, which would have been the first of a new class of super carriers. As well as issues related to the deployment of nuclear weapons, naval aviation faced another challenge in the form of new jet-propelled combat aircraft. Although the Navy was quick to realise their potential, getting them to sea on the existing carriers was another matter. A prototype McDonnell FD (later FH) Phantom flew in January 1945, but it was not until 1948 that a squadron was deployed aboard a carrier, although it was soon apparent that its performance was not that much better than contemporary piston-engined fighters. In practice, it would take several years before improved operational jets such as the Grumman F9F Panther and McDonnell F2H Banshee could be deployed in significant numbers.

Meanwhile, conventional piston-engined aircraft still constituted the major strength of the carrier air groups. The most notable was the Douglas AD Skyraider, which was just entering service when the war ended, while the wartime Vought F4U Corsair continued in production and was to play an important role in the forthcoming Korean War. Also entering service in 1945 was the Grumman F8F Bearcat, which acted as a fast-climbing interceptor that could double as a useful fighter-bomber, although by the start of the Korean War in 1950, most had been relegated to Reserve units.

In terms of aircraft carriers, by 1947 the operational fleet was reduced to eight of the newest Essex class carriers and the three larger Midway class, although even then, three of the Essex were laid up in reserve in 1949 as an economy measure. With the cancellation of the USS *United Sates* and the priority given to the Air Force and its force of nuclear bombers, this period was perhaps the nadir of US naval aviation's fortunes. This situation was about to change dramatically in the new decade ahead.

Opposite: One of the most important new aircraft to enter service just after the war was the Douglas AD-1 Skyraider, which entered front-line service with VA-19A in December 1946. Originally conceived as a single-seat attack aircraft, it proved to be adaptable for many other roles and remained in service until the early 1970s. This example is an early production AD-1, flown by VA-5B aboard the USS *Coral Sea* (CV-43) in 1948. *NARA*

The Skyraider prototype was originally designated as the XBT2D-1 Destroyer II and made its first flight on 18 March 1945. By the time it entered service, the name Skyraider had been adopted and the designation changed to AD-1, reflecting the introduction of the new Attack category, which replaced the wartime Scout and Torpedo Bomber (SB, TB) categories. Eventually, no less than 3,180 Skyraiders had been delivered when production ended in 1957. *NARA*

Opposite: In the late 1940s, the Skyraider rapidly replaced Grumman Avengers and Curtiss Helldivers to become the US Navy's main strike and attack aircraft. As indicated by the letter 'V' on the tail fins, this formation of AD-1s flying over San Diego in 1949 belonged to Carrier Air Group 11 (CVG-11), assigned to the Essex class carrier USS *Valley Forge* (CV-45). *NARA*

In designing the Skyraider, the Douglas team under Ed Heinemann made every effort to save weight and this was the reason why a single-crew configuration was adopted. There was no internal bomb bay and all weapons were carried on underwing hard points. The result was an aircraft that could carry up to 8,000lb of ordnance, as demonstrated here where the load consists of two 500lb bombs, a torpedo, and twelve 5-in rocket projectiles. This particular aircraft is an AD-2 Skyraider, which featured a more powerful engine and a strengthened wing. *NARA*

Above: The Martin Mauler was produced to the same specification as the Skyraider and flew in prototype form as the XBTM-1 on 26 August 1944. Subsequently, an order for 750 BTM-1s was placed on 15 January 1945 although production examples did not fly until almost two years later (December 1946), by which time the aircraft was redesignated in the new Attack category as the AM-1 Mauler. *NARA*

Opposite above: The first Navy squadron to fly the AM-1 Mauler was VA-17A, which received its first aircraft in March 1948, but as from September, it was redesignated VA-174 and was assigned to CVG-17, identified by the tail code R. At one time or another, the Mauler was flown by five front-line squadrons, but its handling qualities left something to be desired and the Navy subsequently decided to standardise on the AD Skyraider. The Maulers were then assigned to Reserve units in 1950 and were finally withdrawn in 1953. *NARA*

Opposite below: At the end of the Pacific War, the principal fighter aboard the Fast Carrier Task Forces was the Grumman F6F Hellcat. However, after the end of hostilities it was rapidly withdrawn from service and replaced by the Grumman F8F-1 Bearcat, shown here. Development of the new fighter had begun in 1943 and the prototype flew on 21 August 1944. Although the Bearcat had the same engine as its predecessor, it was over 2,000lb lighter, and consequently, its rate of climb (4,570ft/min) was almost double that of the Hellcat and it was nearly 50mph faster. *NARA*

Above: Development of the Bearcat was given a high priority as an interceptor to counter the kamikaze attacks, which posed a major threat to the US Navy from October 1944 onwards. However, the first squadron (VF-19) was only equipped in May 1945 and did not see operational service before the end of hostilities. These examples belonging to VF-111 aboard the USS *Valley Forge* (CV-45) in September 1949 are the F8F-2 variant, in which an armament of four 20mm cannon replaced the six 0.5-in machine guns carried by most of the earlier F8F-1s. *NARA*

Opposite above: A total of 1,135 Bearcats were delivered including sixty of the F8F-2P photographic reconnaissance version shown here. Bearcat production ended in May 1949, by which time it equipped a total of twenty-four US Navy squadrons. However, almost immediately, it began to be withdrawn from front-line squadrons and the last operational versions were in fact the photographic F8F-2Ps, which survived until towards the end of 1952. Although replaced by the new breed of jet fighters, the Bearcat had a much shorter take-off run and its initial rate of climb was much better than the slow-accelerating jets. *NARA*

Opposite below: Although deliveries of the Vought F4U Corsair began in late 1942, it was not until mid-1944 that it began to equip squadrons aboard the Essex class carriers of the Pacific Fleet. However, it then showed its worth, shooting down 2,140 enemy aircraft for the loss of only 189 Corsairs. After the war, in contrast to the contemporary Hellcat, it remained in service and further orders were placed for versions of the improved F4U-5 so that the last Corsair only rolled off the production lines as late as December 1952. *NARA*

Above: The F4U-5 Corsair was primarily intended as a high-performance fighter-bomber and could carry up to 4,000lb of bombs or other ordnance. It was also produced as the F4U-5N night fighter, which was equipped with an AN/APS-19 radar carried in a pod on the leading edge of the starboard wing, as illustrated in this example operated by the NATC (Naval Air Test Centre) at NAS Patuxent River. Corsairs were extensively deployed in the Korean War, both on board carriers and with land-based USMC squadrons, for which a specialised ground-attack version was produced as the AU-1, and some of these remained in service until 1957. *NARA*

Opposite above: By the end of the Pacific War the US Navy had commissioned a total of seventeen 27,000-ton Essex class aircraft carriers and another six were subsequently completed. Although several were laid up in reserve, the Essex class continued to be the main platform for the deployment of US Navy air power until towards the end of the 1950s. This is the USS *Kearsarge* (CV-33), which commissioned on 2 March 1946, anchored off Hawaii in April 1948. The aircraft of CVG-33 ranged on deck present an interesting insight into the state of US naval aviation at the time. Aft are Curtiss SB2C Helldivers of VA-3A and Grumman TBM-3E Avengers (configured for the ASW role) of VA-4A, while forward are Grumman F8F Bearcats. This was one of the last deployments of the Helldiver, which was finally withdrawn in 1949. *NARA*

Opposite below: The last Essex class carrier to be commissioned was the USS *Oriskany* (CV-34), but this did not occur until 25 September 1950. The delay was due to the fact that the ship was completed to a modified design (SCB-27A) which incorporated changes to accommodate the operation of jet aircraft. These included the installation of more powerful catapults, jet blast deflectors, removal of the deck-mounted 5-in guns, and a revised island superstructure in which the funnel was faired into the mast and bridge structure. *NARA*

Above: British wartime experience with the Illustrious class carriers constructed with armoured flight decks convinced the US Navy to incorporate this feature in the three new Midway class carriers ordered in 1942. As completed, these ships displaced over 47,000 tons (standard), and an air group of 137 aircraft (73 Bearcats, 64 Helldivers) was planned. The first of these (USS *Midway*, CVB-41) commissioned on 10 September 1945, just too late to see combat action against Japan. *NARA*

Opposite above: The second Midway class was the USS *Franklin D. Roosevelt* (CVB-42), which commissioned at Brooklyn Navy Yard on 27 October 1945. The normal ship's complement was around 2,500 men, most of whom are here lined up on deck to witness the commissioning ceremony. The ship was the first carrier to be named after a US president, but the policy has been revived in recent times with some of the Nimitz class nuclear-powered carriers. Notable in this view is the battery of 5-in/38cal DP guns in single mountings below the flight deck and numerous 40mm and 20mm AA guns in the stern galleries. *NHHC*

Opposite below: With the end of hostilities, construction of the third Midway class, USS *Coral Sea* (CVB-43), was not hurried and she did not commission until 1 October 1947. In this view, taken while working up early in 1948, some eighty aircraft of her air group (CVBG-5) are lined up on deck and consist almost entirely of F4U Corsair fighter-bombers and AD Skyraider attack aircraft. At the time of their entry into service, the Midway class were designated as CVB (Battle Aircraft Carrier) and the air group designation followed suit. In 1952, the ships were redesignated as CVA (Attack Aircraft Carrier). *NARA*

Above: The advent of the atomic bomb was perceived to have completely changed the nature of warfare and the US Navy was determined to have the means to deliver the new weapons. Given the size of the early nuclear weapons (10 tons), a large 45-ton bomber was projected and this necessitated a purpose-built carrier, which, at a displacement of 66,850 tons, was considerably larger than the Midway class. This would be the USS *United States* (CVA-58), shown in this artist's impression, which was intended to carry twenty-four nuclear bombers. The flight deck was completely flush and four catapults were provided, two in the bow and one angled out on either beam amidships. *NARA*

Opposite above: In 1945, the US Navy issued a specification for a carrier-based bomber capable of carrying a 10,000lb bomb load, which resulted in the North American AJ-1 Savage. This is the prototype XAJ-1, which flew on 3 July 1948. By that time, the new Mk.4 nuclear bomb was available and so the Savage, with a loaded weight of around 25 tons, was considerably smaller than the 45-ton bomber originally envisaged. The AJ-1 employed a mixed-power propulsion system with two 2,400hp radial piston engines and single tail-mounted J33 turbojet, which together gave a maximum speed of 471mph and a range of just over 1,500nm. As completed, the USS *United States* was planned to have an air group of eighteen AJ-1 Savages and no less than fifty-four F2H Banshee jet fighters to act as escorts. *NMNA*

Opposite below: The first atomic bombs had been delivered by B-29 Superfortress bombers of the US Army Air Force, which, in September 1947, became the independent United States Air Force. The young service immediately claimed responsibility for the nation's nuclear strike force using the new long-range Convair B-36. This is an early production B-36B, powered by six 3,500hp radial piston engines, which entered service with SAC in 1948. In the meantime, a vicious political battle broke out behind the scenes as the Air Force and Navy fought over the necessary funds for their nuclear strike projects. The keel of the USS *United States* was laid down on 14 April 1949, but construction was terminated only five days later when a controversial decision in favour of the USAF and their B-36 was made by the Secretary of Defense. *NARA*

Above: Despite the cancellation of the *United States*, the US Navy was still working on the concept of launching nuclear strikes from existing aircraft carriers. The purpose-designed AJ Savage would not be in service until at least 1950, but in the meantime, a version of the Neptune land-based patrol bomber, designated P2V-3C, was adapted for the role. With gun turrets removed to save weight and increased internal fuel tankage, the Neptune could take off from the deck of a Midway class carrier using JATO rockets, as in this early trial from the *Midway* (CVB-41) on 7 April 1949. Configured for carrier operations, the Neptune demonstrated a range of 5,000nm, more than enough to reach Moscow from the central Mediterranean, where the carriers were deployed. *NARA*

Opposite above: The JATO assisted take-offs were dramatic affairs, as shown in this Neptune being launched from the USS *Franklin D. Roosevelt* (CVB-42). However, there was no question of a landing back aboard the carriers and a return would have to be made to a suitable land airfield if the aircraft had survived its perilous mission. The first modified Neptunes were allocated to VC-5 and were deployed to NAS Port Lyautey, Morocco, from where they would be craned aboard the carriers when required. The Little Boy nuclear weapons were stored aboard the carriers. The squadron was also equipped with the new AJ Savage, but these were plagued with serviceability issues, which were not resolved until late 1951, after which the Neptunes were progressively withdrawn. *NARA*

Opposite below: Another issue that challenged US naval aviation in the late 1940s was adapting the new jet engine technology to carrier-borne fighters and attack aircraft. An early step was taken with the Ryan FR-1 Fireball, which featured a mixed-power layout with a 1,350hp Wright Cyclone radio piston engine in the nose and a General Electric J31 turbojet mounted in the tail. One squadron, VF-66 (later redesignated VF-41), was just becoming operational in August 1945 when the war ended and large production contracts were cancelled, only sixty-six FR-1s being delivered. The squadron conducted trials off several carriers (image shows a Fireball launching from the escort carrier USS *Badoeng Strait* in 1947), but as result of some accidents, including at least one structural failure, the Fireball was withdrawn from service in 1947 and most of the airframes were scrapped. *NMNA*

Above: The McDonnell XFD-1 Phantom first flew on 26 January 1945 and subsequently made the first landing by a US pure jet aircraft aboard an aircraft carrier (USS *Franklin D. Roosevelt*) on 21 July 1946. Sixty production Phantoms (now designated FH-1) were delivered in 1947/48 and the first squadron to be equipped was VF-17A, which briefly embarked in the USS *Saipan* (CVL-48) to allow its pilots to become carrier qualified. It thus became the first operational jet fighter squadron to be deployed at sea, although not as a permanent component of the ship's air group. Although it gave the US Navy early experience of operating jets, the Phantom's limited performance meant that it was quickly replaced by later and more capable jet fighters. *ASM*

Opposite above: As the US Navy evaluated the potential of the new jets, its next example was the North American FJ-1 Fury. This was a compact design powered by a single 4,000lb.s.t. J35 turbojet, giving it a maximum speed of 547mph and initial rate of climb of 3,300ft/min (substantially less than the piston-engined Bearcat). The first of three prototypes flew on 27 November 1946, but subsequently, only thirty were ordered. However, these were sufficient to equip VF-5A (later VF-51), which carried out trials aboard the Essex class carrier USS *Boxer* (CV-21) in March 1948. For a few months in 1949, the squadron deployed as an integral part of the ship's air group. Thereafter, the aircraft were allocated to Naval Reserve units including that based at NAS Oakland, whose pilots demonstrate a tight formation in early 1950. The FJ-1 was finally retired 1953. *NMNA*

Opposite below: The most successful of the early naval jet fighters was the Grumman F9F Panther, which equipped many operational squadrons and was to play an important role in the forthcoming Korean War. The prototype XF9F-2 flew on 24 November 1947 and was powered by a 5,000lb.s.t. Pratt & Whitney J42 turbojet, a licence-built vision of the Rolls-Royce Nene. The first squadron to receive the new fighters was VF-17A, which in 1949 traded in its earlier FH-1 Phantoms, against which the Panther was 100mph faster and had a substantially greater range. These F9F-2s are deployed aboard the USS *Midway* (CVB-41) and appear to be attracting a lot of interest from the ship's crew. *NARA*

Chapter 2

The Korean War
1950-1953

In the closing stages of the Pacific War, with the Japanese fleet virtually annihilated, the emphasis of carrier operations began to shift to attacks against land targets, either in support of ground troops in action or against more strategic targets such as factories. Events in the Korean War were to establish this as the carrier's prime role, enshrined in the concept of power projection, whereby the carriers provided mobile bases for the constant application of naval air power in support of operations ashore.

At 4 a.m. (local time) on 25 June 1950, North Korean forces poured across the 38th parallel and quickly overwhelmed the unprepared South Korean army. By early September, they had occupied almost the whole of South Korea, with beleaguered US and UN forces stubbornly holding out in a small area in the south-eastern tip of the Korean mainland, which became known as the Pusan Pocket. It was a desperate situation. The North Korean invasion came as a complete surprise to the United States government and military establishment. The US Navy had no carriers in Korean waters, but the Essex class USS *Valley Forge* was quickly deployed with the British carrier HMS *Triumph* and, together with escorting cruisers and destroyers, they formed Task Force 77 Striking Group. The first of a series of attacks against North Korean airfields and ground forces on the west coast was launched on 3 July. This was only eight days after the start of hostilities and served as a graphic illustration of the flexibility of carrier air power. Another example was that, being offshore close to potential targets, the carrier aircraft could carry heavy loads of bombs and rockets compared to the USAF aircraft based in Japan (the jet-powered P-80s could only manage two 100lb bombs).

To relieve the situation, the UN C-in-C, General Douglas MacArthur, devised a bold masterstroke and launched a successful amphibious landing at Inch'on on the Korean west coast, just south of the 38th parallel. This cut through the Communist supply lines and together with reinforcements breaking out of the Pusan Pocket, the North Korean army was forced to retreat almost back to the Manchurian border by early November 1950. However, at that point, massive Chinese forces entered the war and forced the UN forces to retreat so that by January 1951, they again occupied substantial areas of South Korea. Eventually they were pushed back and by May 1951, a relatively stable front line had been established roughly corresponding to the 38th parallel, where it remained, with variations, until the signing of the armistice on 27 July 1953.

From the start, the aircraft carriers played a significant role in the war, which dragged on for three years. At times, the US Navy had four fleet carriers operating off the Korean coast, supported by several escort and support carriers. Just before the outbreak of war, the US Navy had begun to equip its fighter squadrons with the F9F Panther jet fighter, which was soon in action; although experience was to prove that it was no match for the swept-wing MiG-15, which appeared with the Chinese involvement in November 1950. This experience was to drive the development of a new generation of swept-wing fighters for the US Navy, but none were in action before the end of hostilities.

When North Korean troops crossed the 38th parallel and invaded South Korea on 25 June 1950, the nearest available US Navy carrier was the Essex class USS *Valley Forge* (CV-45). It was immediately directed to Okinawa, where it met up with the British light fleet carrier HMS *Triumph* and together with supporting warships they formed Task Force 77. On 3 July, they launched the first strikes against Korean targets. *Valley Forge's* air group (CAG-5) comprised two squadrons of F9F Panther jet fighters, two squadrons of F4U Corsair fighter-bombers and one squadron of AD Skyraider attack bombers. *NHHC*

Above: A Grumman F9F-3 Panther of VF-52 'Knightriders' aboard the USS *Valley Forge* being prepared for a strike mission on 19 July 1950. This version of the Panther was powered by a 4,600lb.s.t. Allison J33 turbojet and fifty-four examples were ordered. However, the Navy decided to standardise on the more powerful Pratt & Whitney J42 and all F9F-3s were eventually converted to F9F-2 standard. At this time, the ship's air group (CVG-5) was engaged in operations to support a US Army landing at P'ohang just north of Pusan, at the south-east tip of South Korea. *NHHC*

Opposite above: On 1 August 1950, Task Force 77 was reinforced by the arrival of the Essex Class USS *Philippine Sea* (CV-47) with its embarked air group (CAG-11) of Panthers, Corsairs and Skyraiders. Between operations the carriers were based at Sasebo in Japan, where the *Philippine Sea* is shown during January 1951 with other ships of the US 7th Fleet in the background. On deck aft are the AD-4 Skyraiders of VA-115 and F4U-4B Corsairs of VF-113 and VF-114. On the forward deck park are more Corsairs and a few F9F-2 Panthers of VF-111 and VF-112. *NHHC*

Opposite below: The Douglas AD Skyraider proved to be one of the most useful naval aircraft in the Korean War. It could carry a heavy ordnance load, had a longer range and was less vulnerable to ground fire than the F4U Corsair. This AD-4 belonging to VA-115 aboard USS *Philippine Sea* (CV-47) is being armed in preparation for a strike on Korea's east coast in support of United Nations troops. The aircraft is in the process of being armed with Load Baker, which consists of twelve 250lb fragmentation bombs and will include three 150-gallon napalm bombs and 200 rounds for each of the two wing-mounted 20mm cannon. In this configuration, the Skyraider would have an endurance of four hours. *NARA*

Above: The most numerous combat aircraft deployed aboard the US carriers during the Korean War was the Vought F4U Corsair. It was used almost exclusively in the ground-attack and close air support (CAS) roles, notably by many USMC squadrons. In such operations, it proved superior to the USAF Mustangs as it could carry a much greater ordnance load and its air-cooled radial engine was less prone to battle damage than the latter's in-line liquid-cooled engines with their vulnerable cooling systems. This F4U-4B belonging to Marine squadron VMF-214 aboard the USS *Sicily* (CVE-118) is being readied for a strike against North Korean forces in August 1950. The weapon load includes eight HVAR, each with a hitting power equivalent to a 5-in gun shell, as well as a 1,000lb bomb, while under the starboard centre section is a 150-gallon fuel tank. This combination was known as Load Able. *NHHC*

Opposite above: The previous photo of the Corsair was taken aboard the USS *Sicily*, one of two wartime escort carriers that reached Korean waters in early August 1950. The other was the USS *Badoeng Strait* (CVE-116) and each carried a USMC squadron equipped with twenty-four F4U-4/5 Corsairs. This photo shows *Badoeng Strait* off Korea in January 1952, at which time she had VMF-212 embarked and a four-ship section of their Corsairs has just landed on. *NHHC*

Opposite below: The next Essex class carrier to reach Korean waters was the USS *Boxer* (CV-21). Her first task following the outbreak of war was to ferry a load of 145 P-51 Mustangs together with the supporting personnel and equipment from California to Japan. In this view, she is leaving San Francisco on 14 July 1950 with her after flight deck occupied by dozens of the Mustangs. After a very quick return voyage, she departed again from California on 24 August with CAG-5 embarked, which comprised four squadrons of F4U Corsairs and one of AD Skyraiders. She joined Task Force 77 just in time to support the landings at Inchon in September. *NARA*

Above: The carriers of TF.77 played a vital part in supporting the landings at Inchon on 15 September 1950, and during the next two weeks, the three Essex class carriers flew 2,249 sorties while even the two small escort carriers managed another 840. The scale of this very successful operation can be gauged from this view of part of the invasion fleet being overflown by a Corsair of VF-113 from USS *Philippine Sea* (CV-47). Immediately below the Corsair is the battleship USS *Missouri* (BB-63) and in the background are many of the troopships and transports involved. *NHHC*

Opposite above: The principal jet fighter embarked on the US carriers was the Grumman F9F-2 Panther. Operating them from unmodified Essex class carriers wasn't easy and there were strict limitations on the amount of ordnance they could carry. Initially, only some of the Essex class embarked a single F9F squadron, but by 1953, most had two squadrons and at one point, the *Bunker Hill* (CV-21) operated three jet squadrons. In the air the Panther was, in theory, outclassed by the swept-wing Mig-15, but better training and tactics made up for the difference in performance to some extent. A greater threat was the intense North Korean AA fire, which accounted for a total of fifty-seven Panthers during the war. This F9F-2 is flown by VF-24 operating off *Bunker Hill* (CV-21) as part of CVG-2 in 1952. *NARA*

Opposite below: A second jet fighter deployed by the US Navy in the Korean War was the McDonnell F2H-2 Banshee. Popularly known as the 'Banjo', it was a substantial development of the FH-1 Phantom and flew in prototype form (XF2H-1) as early as 11 January 1947 (before the Panther had flown). Compared to the Panther, the production F2H-2 was larger and heavier, and was powered by twin 3,250lb.s.t. J34 turbojets. Consequently, it was more expensive, which was the main reason the Navy standardised on the Grumman fighter. However, it was liked by the pilots, who appreciated the security offered by two engines, and it performed better at high altitudes. This example shown over Wonsan in late 1952 was flown by VF-11 embarked on the USS *Kearsarge* (CV-33). *NARA*

Above: A pair of F2H-2 Banshees overflying the ships of Task Force 77 shortly after the signing of the armistice on 27 July 1953, which brought active combat operations to an end. They are flown by VF-22 embarked on the USS *Lake Champlain* (CV-39), whose air group CVG-4 also included the Banshee-equipped VF-62. In the later stages of the war, US Navy jet fighters were often tasked with escorting formations of USAF B-29 bombers, and with their better high altitude performance, the Banshees provided top cover while the Panthers operated at lower altitudes. *NARA*

Opposite above: The USS *Lake Champlain* had been laid up in reserve in 1947, but following the start of the Korean War she was taken in hand for a refit and update to SCB-27A standard to allow the operation of jet fighters. This was not completed until September 1952, and consequently, she only carried out a single operational deployment to Korea, which began in April 1953, but from mid-June was in continuous action until the signing of the armistice. Apart from the two squadrons of F2H-2 Banshee fighter-bombers, she also carried a nuclear-capable detachment (VC-4 with F2H-2Bs) and a photoreconnaissance detachment (VC-61 with F2H-2Ps). *NARA*

Opposite below: The F2H-2P was the photographic reconnaissance version of the Banshee and was distinguished by a lengthened nose containing K-38 cameras with a 36-inch focal length, which enabled detailed images to be taken from an altitude of 15,000 feet. The F2H-2P was the most successful PR aircraft deployed in the Korean War and detachments served aboard most of the Essex class carriers involved. Note that this example does not carry wingtip tanks, which were normally fitted. However, deck crews could not fold the wings if the tanks were full (this applied to all F2H variants) and this could create problems for the flight deck aircraft handlers. *NARA*

Opposite above: A pair of F4U-5N Corsair night fighters overflying the carrier USS *Boxer* (CV-21) in September 1951, shortly before the ship was involved in supporting Operation Chromite (the successful amphibious assault at Inchon, which was launched on 15 September 1950). Two other Essex class carriers were involved in this operation (USS *Philippine Sea*, USS *Valley Forge*), but whereas these each embarked two squadrons of Panther jets, *Boxer's* air group (CVG-2) had none. Instead, it included no less than four F4U-4 fighter-bomber squadrons, an F4U-5N night fighter detachment (VC-3), and a photoreconnaissance detachment (VC-61) flying F4U-4P Corsairs. *Boxer* was one of the most active Task Force 77 carriers, making no less than four operational deployments during the Korean War. *NHHC*

Opposite below: Although the jets did useful work in Korea as fighter-bombers, they were limited in the amount of ordnance they could carry (at best a pair of 1,000lb bombs) and were restricted in the time they could spend over a target due to their limited fuel endurance. The Navy's most effective attack bomber was the piston-engined Douglas AD Skywarrior, which routinely carried up to 8,000lb of ordnance and could remain on call over a target for several hours. These AD-2 Skyraiders of VA-702 were based aboard USS *Boxer* in the summer of 1951. Significantly, the squadron was a Reserve unit, as indeed were all the other squadrons in the ship's air group at the time. *NARA*

Skyraiders were also responsible for one of the most famous attacks during the Korean War. The target was the Hwachon Dam, which controlled the flow of the Pukhan River, and as UN forces advanced northwards, their progress could be halted by opening the dam's sluices and flooding the plains below. If some of the sluice gates could be destroyed, then the Communist's ability to control the water flow would be lost. Following an earlier failed attack with bombs and rockets, the USS *Princeton* (CV-37) launched eight Skyraiders from VA-195 and VC-35, each armed with Second World War vintage Mk.13 torpedoes. Seven of the eight hit their intended targets (although one failed to explode), destroying one sluice gate and severely damaging another, as can be seen in this dramatic action photo. VA-195 subsequently had no hesitation in claiming the title 'Dambusters'! *NHHC*

Opposite: Korea suffered from severe winter conditions throughout the war, as illustrated in this view of aircraft ranged aboard the carrier USS *Philippine Sea* (CV-47) in late January 1952. In the foreground are F9F-2 Panthers of VF-112, which was the only jet squadron embarked apart from a detachment of VC-61 equipped with a mix of PR Panthers and Banshees. The rest of the air group (CVG-11) was made up of two squadrons of F4U-4 Corsairs and one of AD-4 Skyraiders, together with specialised night fighter and AEW detachments. In these conditions, keeping the flight deck clear for flight operations, de-icing the aircraft, and carrying out routine maintenance in sub-zero conditions was a nightmare for the crew. *NHHC*

During the Second World War, the US Navy developed and refined the concept of a fleet train, which enabled its carrier task forces to remain at sea for long periods. This capability was again needed in the Korean War to keep the ships of Task Force 77 continuously on station. Here the USS *Princeton* (CV-37) and a Gearing class destroyer take on stores from a fleet supply tanker in the summer of 1952. On the carrier's flight deck are Skyraiders of VA-195 and Corsairs of VF-192 and VF-193. An interesting detail is that the two aircraft parked right forward on the port side are Grumman TBM-3R Avengers. Although obsolete as a torpedo bomber, the -3R was a modified seven-passenger variant for the COD role. *NARA*

Above: The Douglas F3D Skyknight was the first purpose-designed naval jet night fighter. First flown on 23 March 1948, production examples of the uprated F3D-2 reached the first US Navy squadron (VC-3) in 1951. Although designed to operate from carriers, only a few were deployed at sea including this example belonging to VC-4, which conducted brief trials aboard the USS *Franklin D. Roosevelt* (CVA-42) in 1952. Instead, the F3D-2 equipped two land-based USMC squadrons in Korea, where they proved surprisingly effective in their designed role. In fact, the Skyknight was responsible for shooting down more enemy aircraft than any other Navy or Marine fighter. *NHHC*

Opposite above: While the Essex class carriers bore the brunt of the naval air war over Korea, during the same period the new large Midway class carriers were deployed in turn to the US Navy's 6th Fleet operating in the Mediterranean and Atlantic. Although the war in Korea dominated, the threat of a worldwide nuclear conflict was always present. Cruising in the Mediterranean, the embarked P2V Neptune and AJ Savage nuclear-capable bombers were placed in range of key Soviet targets such as Moscow itself. The carriers also participated in major exercises in the North Atlantic with the newly formed NATO. USS *Midway* (CVB-41) is shown here while participating in Exercise Mainbrace in September 1952. *NHHC*

Opposite below: The AJ-1 Savages were normally based ashore in Morocco but deployed aboard carriers when the situation required. The smaller Essex class carriers proved capable of operating the Savage and this example has just landed on the USS *Wasp* (CVA-18), while the latter passed through the Mediterranean in 1954 during the course of an east-about world cruise. With a wingspan of just over 75 feet (excluding the wing tanks), the big bomber was a tight fit on the 96ft wide flight deck of the unmodified Essex class. *NHHC*

The appearance of the MiG-15 led to an urgent requirement for a swept-wing naval fighter of similar performance. In fact, a solution was in hand and a prototype swept-wing derivative of the Panther, redesignated as the F9F-6 Cougar, was flown as early as 20 September 1951. It was powered by an uprated version of the J48 turbojet, which had powered the Panther, and this, together with the swept wing, resulted in a maximum speed of 690mph, which was over 100mph faster than its predecessor. However, by the time testing and evaluation was completed, the first squadron (VF-32) was not formed until November 1952. *NHHC*

Opposite: The first Cougar-equipped squadron to deploy as part of a carrier air group (CVG-2 in this case) was VF-24 aboard the carrier USS *Yorktown* (CVA-10), which had been recommissioned as an attack carrier in February 1953 after a period in reserve. Subsequently, the ship joined Task Force 77 off Korea in August 1953, just too late for the new jets to see combat action. Between June 1952 and January 1953, *Yorktown* had been refitted to SCB-27A standards and this had included the installation of a pair of 210ft H8 catapults and rudimentary jet blast deflectors. These modifications can be seen here as the Cougars of VF-24, which adopted the name 'Corsairs', prepare for launching in August 1953. *USN*

Another swept-wing naval fighter that was rapidly developed as a result of experience in Korea was the North American FJ-2 Fury. This was a naval version of the Air Forces's F-86 Sabre, which itself, ironically, was developed from the earlier naval straight-winged FJ-1 Fury (see Chapter 1). The first of three XFJ-2 prototypes, flown on 27 December 1951, was basically an F-86E fitted with an arrester hook and catapult points. The other two also had a lengthened nose wheel strut to increase the angle of attack at take-off and one of these is shown aboard the USS *Coral Sea* (CVB-43) carrying out initial carrier trials in December 1952. Too late for the Korean War, the production FJ-2s were all allocated to USMC squadrons, starting in January 1954. It was not until September of that year that naval units began re-equipping with the FJ-3, in which the more powerful J65 replaced the J47 turbojet in the FJ-2. *NARA*

Chapter 3

Supersonics and Supercarriers
1954-1965

One of the most significant aspects of the Korean War was that it did not trigger an all-out nuclear war as many had expected. Consequently, it quickly became obvious that, even in the atomic era, aircraft carriers still had an important role to play in the furtherance of US policy and objectives. This was shown clearly by the actions of the carriers and their air groups. Not only did they provide highly professional support to ground troops in action, they also mounted interdiction campaigns to halt or slow down supplies to the Communist front-line forces and also attacked strategic targets such as factories, generating stations and even dams! Despite the difficulties of countering the highly effective MiG-15s, Navy pilots co-operated with the Air Force in the establishment of air superiority over the Korean Peninsula to the extent that UN ground forces experienced only a small fraction of the weight of air attack made on the enemy troops. One classic operation was the protection afforded to the US Marines X Corps, which was surrounded near Chosin reservoir as Chinese forces advanced in November 1950. Despite overwhelming Chinese strength occupying a potential withdrawal route, the majority of the 14,000 troops involved made their way safely to the east coast port of Hungnam, from where they were evacuated together with their arms and equipment. In the course of this action over eleven days, the Marines lost 718 men, but it was estimated that the Chinese lost the equivalent of seven divisions due to the continuous deprivations of Navy and Marine Corsairs and Skyraiders.

These and other actions of the carriers and their air groups quickly revised political opinion in regard to their usefulness and, as a result, the Navy was authorised to begin the construction of a new class of four 'super carriers'. Displacing over 60,000 tons, they were considerably larger than the earlier Midway class and the longer and wider flight deck enabled the operation of the new breed of swept-wing jet fighters that began to enter service just as the Korean War ended. The ability to handle high-performance jets was further enhanced by the adoption of a number advances pioneered by the British Royal Navy which included the angled deck, steam catapults and mirror landing sights. The first of the new 65,000-ton Forrestal class carriers commissioned in 1955 and all four were in service by the end of the decade. They were followed by three similar Kitty Hawk class, which commissioned between 1961 and 1965 (followed by the improved USS *John F. Kennedy* in 1968). In 1958, the Navy's first fully supersonic fighter, the F8U Crusader, entered service and was followed in the early 1960s by the first versions of the legendary F-4 Phantom. Thus, in the decade following the Korean War, US naval aviation was transformed and expanded so that when it became involved in another Asian war in the 1960s it was in a much better shape to take on the missions with which it was to be tasked.

The US Navy was quick to adopt the British idea of an angled deck and the Essex class carrier USS *Antietam* (CV-36) was selected to undergo a trial conversion. In September 1952 she entered the New York Naval Yard for the work to be carried out and this was completed by the end of the year. The great advantage of the angled deck was that aircraft that missed the arrester wires could safely take off again over the port side of the ship, avoiding the previously all too frequent crash into a crowded forward deck park. Shown here as converted (now designated CVA-36), it is noticeable that the deck-edge lift, a standard feature on the Essex class, is retained even though it would stop landings taking place when in use. *NHHC*

Some of the pilots involved in the angled deck trials discuss the issues arising. Note that at this stage the US Navy referred to the concept as the 'canted deck'. The trials were an outstanding success and in June 1953, the ship crossed the Atlantic to allow the Royal Navy to experience the new method of carrier flight deck operations. During two days of demonstrations, Royal Navy Seahawks and Attackers made numerous take-offs and landings to allow a cross-section of its pilots to evaluate the flight deck configuration. *NARA*

The *Antietam* conversion was a one-off and the SCB-27A improvements already incorporated in some other carriers were not included in order to expedite the completion of the new angled deck. However, three other Essex class that had commenced or were about to commence reconstruction to SCB-27C standards were modified to a new SCB-125 standard. Apart from the angled deck, this involved fitting of a so-called 'hurricane' bow, new and stronger arrester gear with only four wires, a larger forward lift and a new deck-edge lift aft of the island superstructure, and (most importantly) the installation of steam catapults. This photo shows USS *Bon Homme Richard* (CVA-31) after her reconstruction, which was completed in September 1955. *NARA*

SCB-110 was the designation given to the reconstruction of the three large Midway class carriers, which was along similar lines to the Essex class SCB-125 programme. The first to be taken in hand, in April 1954, was the USS *Franklin D. Roosevelt* (now CVA-42) and this photo shows her in April 1956 after she recommissioned. Visible changes include the angled deck and a new deck-edge lift on the starboard side. The USS *Midway* (CVA-41) was similarly modernised and work was completed in 1957. The third ship, USS *Coral Sea* (CVA-43), underwent a more extensive SCB-110A refit and this was not completed until January 1960. *NARA*

The undeniable usefulness of the US Navy's carriers in the opening stages of the Korean War resulted in Congressional approval for the design and construction of a new large carrier, which was laid down on 14 July 1952 as the USS *Forrestal* (CVA-59). Named after James Forrestal, the US Secretary of Defense who had fought the Navy's case for new large aircraft carriers, the ship commissioned in October 1955. The advantages of the angled deck concept as evidenced by trials with the USS *Antietam* resulted in the adoption of the new configuration and allowed room for a conventional island superstructure on the starboard side. This view shows the ship shortly after completion and points of note include the three deck-edge lifts, and on deck is a Douglas XF4D-1 Skyray delta-winged fighter, then undergoing flight testing. *NARA*

The sheer size of the Forrestal class (60,000 tons standard displacement) was due to the desire to maintain the strength of the air group at around eighty to ninety aircraft at a time when they, in turn, were getting larger and heavier and were requiring greater quantities of fuel and ordnance to be embarked. In particular, the Navy had developed a new jet nuclear bomber in the form of the Douglas A3D Skywarrior, which first flew in October 1952. Design work had started in the immediate aftermath of the cancellation of CVA-58 and the intention was that it would operate from the Midway class carriers. However, the larger Forrestal class could accommodate them more safely and in greater numbers. This is an early example of the main production version (A3D-2), which entered service in 1956 and is finished in the then recently introduced grey/white colour scheme. *NARA*

The capability of the USS *Forrestal* is shown in this view of the ship while on her first deployment in January 1957 with the Mediterranean-based US 6th Fleet. On deck are ranged some aircraft of her air group (CVG-1), which includes six A3D Skywarrior nuclear-capable bombers (one in front of the island and another five further aft) of VAH-1 'Smokin' Tigers'. On the bow are AD-6 Skyraiders of VA-15 'Valions', alongside three F3H-2 Demons of VF-14 'Tophatters', while ranged on the angled deck overhang are seven FJ-3 Furies of VF-84 'Vagabonds'. Other aircraft visible aft of the island and on the stern are F9F-6 Cougars and F2H-2P Banshees. *USN*

The decade following the Korean War was a challenging time for US naval aviation with the commissioning of the new supercarriers and the advent of a variety of new aircraft types. Among these was the McDonnell F3H Demon, which had a somewhat chequered history. Although the XF3H-1 was first flown in August 1951, it was powered by the abortive J40 turbojet, and the definitive Allison J71-powered F3H-2 did not fly until 1955 and subsequently only entered front-line service in 1956. This is an F2H-2N radar-equipped all-weather fighter of VF-31 'Tomcatters' aboard the USS *Saratoga* (CVA-60) in 1958. *Saratoga* was the second of the Forrestal class and had commissioned in April 1956. *NMNA*

Above: Later versions of the Demon were equipped to carry AIM-7 Sparrow and/or AIM-9 Sidewinder air-to-air missiles. This pair flown by VF-13 'Night Cappers' operating from the Essex class carrier USS *Shangri-La* (CVA-38) in 1963 are fitted for Sparrow missiles. In fact, between them they encapsulate the history of the F3H Demon. The farthest aircraft (coded 105) was one of the original J40-powered F3H-1s but was later rebuilt to F3H-2 standards with the J71 turbojet. The other (coded 104) is a standard F3H-2 modified to carry the Sparrow missiles, but others, manufactured as missile carriers, were designated F3H-2M. From 1962, these were designed as F-3B or MF-3B respectively, and all Demons had been withdrawn from front-line service by 1965. *NMNA*

Opposite above: Another advanced aircraft that suffered an extended gestation due to issues with the J40 engine was the Douglas F4D Skyray. The prototype XF4D-1 flew in January 1951 but was only powered by an Allison 5,000lb.s.t. J35 turbojet due to non-availability of the intended 7,000lb.s.t. J40. Ultimately, the production F4D-1 had the Pratt & Whitney J57, capable (with afterburner) of 14,500lb.s.t., which endowed the Skyray with a speed of just in excess of Mach 1 at altitude, but more significantly, a spectacular initial rate of climb at 18,000ft/min. Issues experienced during flight testing delayed deliveries to the Navy until 1956 and in that year, a Skyray from the Naval Air Test Centre is here embarked aboard the USS *Forrestal* for carrier trials. *NARA*

Opposite below: The delta-winged Skyray was designed as a deck-launched interceptor that could reach 40,000ft in under four minutes, in time to intercept an inbound bomber before it could get in range to launch an anti-ship missile. Operating successfully in this role it equipped several USN and USMC squadrons, but by 1962, its front-line service was terminated, partly due to its specialised mission making it unadaptable to other roles. This pair of F4D-1 Skyrays are flown by VFAW-3 'Blue Nemisis', which was actually based at NAS North Island as part of the North American Air Defence (NORAD) network. *USN*

Among the many new naval jets that appeared in the early 1950s was the Douglas A4D Skyhawk. Initially known as the 'Bantam Bomber' due to its relatively small size (with a wingspan of only 27ft 6in, it did not need folding wings to fit the standard carrier lifts), a total of 2,960 A4D/A-4 variants were produced between 1954 and 1979. Following the first flight of the XA4D-1 in June 1954, few problems were encountered, and the first deliveries to VA-72 took place in October 1956. This A4D-2 was one of several that re-equipped VA-44 in September 1958 and it displays a representative selection of the ordnance it could carry. Significantly, this includes a Mk.7 nuclear bomb (the large one just to the right of the aircraft's nose). *NMNA*

A busy flight deck scene aboard the USS *Saratoga* (CVA-60), probably around 1960, as the catapult chief prepares to wave off the Skyhawk ready for launching. The aircraft is an A4D-2 (A-4B after 1962) of VA-34 'Blue Blasters', one of the squadrons in the ship's air group (CVG-3). Of particular note is the Mk.7 nuclear store (probably an inert shape), carried on the centreline pylon, and the 250-US gallon fuel tanks under each wing. The total weight of this combination is just over 5,000lb (2,270kg), which represents a full load for an A4D-2. Visible behind the Skyhawk is an A3D-2 Skywarrior of VAH-9, the resident heavy attack squadron. *NMNA*

Above: Despite the widespread adoption of the angled deck, several of the Essex class were never rebuilt to the new configuration and retained their axial flight decks. One of these was the USS *Lake Champlain* (CVA-39), shown here while visiting Cannes in 1957 on deployment with the US 6th Fleet in the Mediterranean with aircraft of ATG-182 ranged on deck. Despite the lack of an angled deck, the ship carries a variety of jet fighters including F9F-8 Cougars of VF-81 'Crusaders', F2H-4 Banshees of VMF-533 'Hawks', and a detachment of VFP-62 flying F9F-8P Cougars. Also on board are Skyraider variants AD-6, AD-5N and AD-5W, as well as the AJ-2 Savages of VAH-7 'Go Devils'. *NARA*

Opposite above: One of the more exotic aircraft aboard US carriers in the 1950s was the Vought F7U Cutlass. Although first flown in 1948, the definitive F7U-3 did not reach operational squadrons until 1954, and while pilots found it generally easy to fly in the air and very manoeuvrable, it had a poor maintenance record and proved to be hazardous to operate aboard the carriers. In fact, all three original XF7U-1 prototypes were lost in crashes, a record that was not improved in service, where a quarter of the 307 Cutlasses delivered were lost in accidents and several pilots killed. Only four squadrons eventually flew the F7U-3 or missile-armed F7U-3M between 1954 and 1957, when the type was withdrawn from front-line service and, in most cases, replaced by the more reliable F9F-8 Cougar. The F7U-3 shown landing aboard the USS *Bon Homme Richard* belongs to VF-212, part of CVG-2 between August 1956 and February 1957. *NARA*

Opposite below: The supercarrier USS *Forrestal* was followed by USS *Saratoga* (CVA-60, commissioned 1956), *Ranger* (CVA-61, 1957) and *Independence* (CVA-62, 1959). The latter is shown here in 1961 refuelling from the fleet tanker USS *Neosho* (AO-143), with the destroyer USS *Dyess* (DDR-880) also in company. On the carrier's deck are aircraft of CVG-7, which include F3H Demons of VF-41 'Black Aces', AD Skyhawks of VA-72, 'Blue Hawks', A3D Skywarriors of VAH-1 'Smokin' Tigers', as well as several AD-6 and AD-5Q Skyraiders. However, the most significant aircraft are the F8U-1 Crusaders of VF-84 'Jolly Rogers', which were coming into widespread use at that time. *NHHC*

Above: The F8U Crusader (designated F-8 after 1962) was the result of a 1952 US Navy specification for a supersonic day fighter, and the XF8U-1 prototype first flew on 25 March 1955. One requirement of the specification was that the landing speed should not exceed 100kts, and this, together with the fact that the swept wing needed a high angle of attack to function at low speeds, led to the adoption of a variable incidence wing mechanism that enabled the pilot to retain a good view over the nose when the aircraft was in a landing configuration. This feature can be seen in this 1958 view of an F8U-1 Crusader of VF-32 'Swordsmen', which has just landed aboard the USS *Saratoga* (CV-60) in 1958. *NMNA*

Opposite above: Flight testing of the Crusader revealed no particular problems, although in service it needed careful handling on approaching to land. VF-32, the first unit to equip with the new fighter, received its first aircraft in March 1957 and subsequently, the Crusader served with around seventy USN and USMC squadrons and remained in front-line service for almost twenty years. During that time, it was constantly upgraded, and this photo shows a pair of F-8E Crusaders of VF-11 'Red Rippers' overflying their parent carrier USS *Franklin D. Roosevelt* (CVA-42). Part of CVG/CVW-1, the squadron and its Crusaders had a long association with this carrier, carrying out nine deployments between 1960 and 1966. *USN*

Opposite below: Conceived as a lightweight supersonic fighter, the Grumman F11F Tiger was loosely descended from the F9F-6 Cougar and the prototype, first flown on 30 July 1954, was actually designated as the YF9F-9. The production F11F-1 entered service with VA-156 'Iron Tigers' in 1956 and subsequently equipped only five front-line squadrons before being withdrawn from 1959 onwards (although some were then utilised as advanced trainers until 1967). This pair are flown by VF-211 'Fighting Checkmates' from the Essex class carrier USS *Lexington* (CVA-16) during a Pacific deployment in 1959. Both are later production versions with an extended nose intended to accommodate an AN/APS-50 radar, although this was never installed. In practice, the Tiger, underpowered and barely supersonic, was outclassed by the contemporary F8U Crusader. *NMNA*

This view taken aboard the USS *Bon Homme Richard* in late 1957, only a few years after the end of the Korean War, illustrates how new high-performance aircraft have replaced the earlier first generation jets. Ranged forward are the missile-armed FJ-3M Furies of VF-51 'Screaming Eagles' and behind them is an F4D-1 Skyray interceptor of VF-141 'Iron Angels'. In the foreground is an HUP-2 Retriever helicopter from a detachment of HU-1 'Pacific Angels'. These squadrons formed part of CVG-5, which also included a squadron of F9F-8 Cougars, one of A3D-2 Skywarriors, and squadrons and detachments of the long-serving AD-5/6 Skyraider. *USN*

Opposite: One of the most significant events in the history of US naval aviation occurred on 25 November 1961, when the nuclear-powered carrier USS *Enterprise* (CVAN-65) was commissioned. At the time, the *Enterprise* was considered the sole example of its type and, in practice, she would be the last new US aircraft carrier to be commissioned for over a decade until the first of the nuclear-powered Nimitz class entered service in 1975. *Enterprise* is shown here in 1962, during her first commission, with CVG-6 embarked. Aircraft included F-8E Crusaders, A-4C Skyhawks and, lined up on the bow, the newly introduced F-4B Phantoms of VF-102 'Diamondbacks'. *USN*

Above: The F-4B Phantom seen in the previous photo was the Navy's latest all-weather supersonic fighter. Originally developed by McDonnell Douglas as a private venture attack aircraft (designated AH-1), at the Navy's request, it was reconfigured as a two-seat all-weather fighter and the prototype XF4H-1 (strictly speaking, named as the Phantom II following on from the original FH-1 Phantom) flew on 27 May 1958. In February 1960, this pre-production YF4H-1 was deployed aboard the USS *Independence* (CVA-62) for carrier suitability trials. The later definitive production F4H-2 (F-4B) featured a re-profiled canopy to give increased headroom for the radar operator and the radome was enlarged and extended to accommodate the upgraded AN/APQ radar. *AA/MD*

Opposite above: The USS *Kitty Hawk* (CVA-63) was the first of four Improved Forrestal class; the first three commissioned between 1961 and 1965, but the fourth (*John F. Kennedy*, CVA-67) was delayed while a debate raged as to whether she should be nuclear-powered. In the end, this was rejected on cost grounds and she commissioned in 1968, although other modifications led to her being considered as a separate class. The most obvious change in the Kitty Hawk class as compared to the earlier Forrestals was the repositioning of the deck-edge lifts. On the starboard side, there were now two forward of the island and one aft, while port side, one was moved aft, where it did not interfere with angled deck operations. This is *Kitty Hawk* in October 1962 and shows aircraft of CVG-11 on deck, including no less than eight A-3D Skywarriors of VAH-13 'Bats'. *USN*

Opposite below: The North American A3J (A-5) Vigilante was designed as a nuclear strike bomber to replace the A3D Skywarrior. A prototype flew on 31 August 1958 and production aircraft began to reach the VAH squadrons in 1961/62. Among these was VAH-3, one of whose aircraft is shown here in late 1961. However, in the early 1960s, the Navy abandoned the carrier-borne nuclear strike role in favour of submarine-launched ICBMs. An improved version of the Vigilante (A3J-2) was adapted as a long-range supersonic reconnaissance aircraft equipped with both optical and electronic surveillance systems. This form became the RA-5C and most of the heavy attack squadrons changed role and were designated RVAH. *NHHC*

This formation is made up of aircraft from CVW-14 based aboard the Kitty Hawk class carrier USS *Constellation* (CVA-64) in 1963. It gives a good idea of a typical air wing composition as the Navy was about to become heavily involved in the Vietnam War. Leading is a Grumman E-1B Tracer (see Chapter 6) of VAW-11 'Early Eleven' followed by a pair of A-1J/H Skyraiders of VA-145 'Swordsmen', and behind them are two A-4C Skyhawks from VA-146 'Blue Diamonds'. Bringing up the rear is an F-4B Phantom (VF-143 'Pukin' Dogs'), an A-3B Skywarrior (VAH-10 'Vikings'), and an F-8E Crusader (VF-141 'Iron Angels'). Whilst impressive, the operation of six different types of aircraft was a logistic nightmare. *NMNA*

Chapter 4

The Vietnam Era
1965-1975

In 1954, the former French colonies of Indochina were recognised formally as the independent states of Laos, Cambodia and Vietnam. Following the Geneva Agreement, the latter was divided into a Communist-held North Vietnam and the US-supported South Vietnam, with a demilitarised zone between them. The Agreement provided for the unification of the two areas following a referendum on the issue to be held in 1956. This didn't happen and subsequently, the North began a concerted military effort to take over the southern Republic of Vietnam. Initially, the US provided material support and military advisors, but the first actual deployment of US Army troops occurred in 1961, and the situation steadily escalated from that point. Although the US Navy was at first only involved in peripheral activities (mainly reconnaissance flights over Vietnam and Laos), it became an active participant in the shooting war following the attack on the destroyer USS *Maddox* in the Gulf of Tonkin on 2 August 1964. Retaliatory air strikes were mounted, which were then followed by nine years of high intensity operations until hostilities ceased in 1973. These included a series of campaigns against targets in North Vietnam, code-named Rolling Thunder I to VI, later followed in 1972/73 by Freedom Train and Linebacker I and II.

The Forrestal and Kitty Hawk class carriers were all powered by conventional steam turbines, but in November 1961, the US Navy commissioned its first nuclear-powered carrier, the USS *Enterprise*. All were involved at one time or another in the Vietnam conflict, which finally ended with the withdrawal of all US forces in 1975. Backing them up were the three Midway class, and some of the now elderly Essex class, most of which had been modernised with angled decks, steam catapults and other updates. Apart from Phantoms and Crusaders, the carrier air groups encompassed a wide variety of aircraft types for the attack role including the A-4 Skyhawk, A-6 Intruder, A-7 Corsair II and A-5 Vigilante. Surprisingly, the piston-engined AD Skywarrior, which first flew in 1945, was still being used in the attack role until 1968.

During the war, US carriers of Task Force 77 operating off Vietnam lost 527 aircraft during combat operations, over half of which were victims of AA fire over North Vietnam. On the other hand, only fifteen were lost in air-to-air combat, while US Navy and Marine pilots shot down sixty MiGs (MiG-15s, -17s, and -21s). When the war started, informed opinion was that the days of aerial dogfighting were over and that long-range missile kills were the way forward. Almost immediately, this was shown to be a false premise, partly because the Rules of Engagement (ROE) required a positive visual identification of an enemy aircraft before it could be attacked. Better training, including the establishment of the Top Gun tactics school, eventually led to much improved results in 1972/73. As far as carriers were concerned, twenty-one (including four Essex class CVS) made a total of eighty-six deployments. Most of these were at Yankee Station in the Gulf of Tonkin, off the North Vietnam coast, although at times, others were deployed to Dixie Station in the South China Sea to support operations in South Vietnam.

In Vietnam, the Vought F-8 Crusader gained a reputation as a 'MiG Killer'. Although it could carry Sidewinder air-to-air missiles, it was the only US Navy fighter for most of the war period to carry a worthwhile gun armament – in this case, four 20mm cannon. Consequently, it was well suited to close-in aerial dogfighting, a form of combat that Navy (and Air Force) planners had thought to be outmoded in the missile age. This F-8E belongs to VF-194 'Red Lightnings', deployed as part of CVW-19 (as indicated by the NM tail code) aboard the Essex class carrier USS *Ticonderoga* (CVA-14) between October 1966 and May 1967. *USN*

Although highly effective as a fighter-bomber, the F-4 had difficulty in countering the North Vietnamese MiGs as it was only armed with air-to-air missiles, which could not always be used to advantage in the type of aerial combat experienced over Vietnam. Although the USAF later introduced the cannon-armed F-4E, naval variants never carried a fixed gun armament, but some USMC aircraft were fitted with a pair of SUU-16 pods for the 20mm Vulcan rotary cannon intended for ground-attack purposes. The F-4B shown here belongs to VF-114, part of CVW-11, aboard the USS *Kitty Hawk* (CVA-63) during the ship's second Vietnam deployment (December 1967 to June 1968). *NARA*

At one time or another, all of the Forrestal and Kitty Hawk class carriers, except for the *John F. Kennedy* (CVA-68), were deployed off Vietnam. One of these, USS *Ranger* (CVA-61), made no less than seven deployments between 1964 and 1973. She was photographed from the Golden Gate Bridge at San Francisco on 4 November 1967 as she departed for her third deployment, with aircraft of CVW-2 ranged on deck. These include, in the foreground, F-4B Phantoms of VF-21, A-6A Intruders of VA-165, A-7A Corsair IIs of VA-147 and A-4C Skyhawks of VA-22. Other aircraft further aft include a pair of E-A Hawkeyes and a single KA-3B Skywarrior while at bottom right is a UH-2A Seasprite helicopter. During this deployment, the air wing lost two Phantoms, a Corsair II and an Intruder to enemy action. *Bill Larkins via WC*.

The aircraft shown aboard the USS *Ranger* in the previous photo included two new attack aircraft, which entered service just before or during the Vietnam War. One of these was the Grumman A-6 Intruder (originally designated A2F), which first flew in April 1960, and by 1964, a total of eighty-three A-6As had been delivered. The first combat deployment of the Intruder was with VA-75 'Sunday Punchers' aboard the USS *Independence* (CVA-62) between June and November 1965. This was the ship's first and only Vietnam deployment and she lost thirteen aircraft to enemy action, including four Intruders. It was not an auspicious combat debut for an aircraft that subsequently played a major role in the war. The A-6A shown here being launched from the USS *Ranger* (CVA-61) belonged to VA-165 'Boomers', which was part of the ship's air wing (CVW-2) for two deployments between November 1967 and May 1969. *NARA*

Above: The other new attack aircraft was the Ling-Temco-Vought (LTV) A-7 Corsair II, produced as a result of a US Navy 1963 specification for light attack aircraft to replace the A-4 Skyhawk. The Corsair II bore an obvious family resemblance to the F-8 Crusader on which it was based. As supersonic speeds were not required, it was powered by a very fuel-efficient non-afterburning TF-30 turbofan and could carry up 15,000lb of ordnance, more than twice that of the Skyhawk. Production A-7As began to reach the Navy in 1966 and the first squadron (VA-147 'Argonauts') was in action off Vietnam from December 1967 aboard the USS *Ranger* (CVA-61). One of its bomb-laden aircraft is here launched off the ship's waist catapult in the following January. *USN*

Opposite above: The A-7E was an upgraded version of the Corsair II powered by a 14,250lb.s.t. Allison TF-41 turbofan (a licence-built version of the Rolls-Royce Spey). It also had a new and improved avionics system for navigation and targeting, and carried M61 20mm rotary cannon instead of the original two fixed single 20mm guns. The A-7E entered service from 1970 onwards and it rapidly replaced the earlier version, many of which were converted to two-seat TA-7C trainers. This A-7E of VA-146 'Blue Diamonds' is landing aboard the USS *America* (CVA-66) during the type's first operational deployment in May 1970. Note the AIM-9 Sidewinder AAM on a fuselage pylon just under the wing's leading edge. *NARA*

Opposite below: Most Navy jet fighters were also adapted for use as photoreconnaissance aircraft. The RF-8A was the original PR version of the Crusader in which the fixed armament of four 20mm cannon was replaced by a five-camera installation. At the time of the Vietnam War, several were upgraded to F-8G status with strengthened wings and fuselage, ventral fins, upgraded navigation system and an improved camera installation. This is an F-8G of Detachment G, VFP-63 'Eyes of the Fleet', aboard the USS *Oriskany* (CVA-34) in the summer of 1966 during the ship's second Vietnam deployment. The Crusader's high speed and good manoeuvrability made it suitable for low-level tactical reconnaissance missions although, even so, one of VFP-63's aircraft was lost to enemy fire during this deployment. *USN*

Above: As the US Navy abandoned the concept of a carrier-based nuclear strike force, the North American A-5A Vigilante was no longer required as a bomber. However, its long range and high-altitude performance made it ideal for the photoreconnaissance mission and a prototype RA-5C flew on 30 January 1962. Subsequently, ninety-one of this version were delivered, while forty-three of the earlier A-5A bombers were converted to the same standard. The aircraft seen here is one of the converted A-5As and is serving with RVAH-13 'Bats' aboard the USS *Kitty Hawk* (CVA-63) on that ship's first Vietnam deployment between November 1965 and June 1966. At that time the Navy was experimenting with a camouflage finish for its combat aircraft and several of the carrier's air wing (CVW-11) aircraft were painted in dark green jungle colours, including this RF-5C (note also the camouflaged A-1H Skyraider in the background). *USN*

Opposite above: The forward deck park aboard the USS *Constellation* during a 1967 Vietnam deployment contains an interesting selection of aircraft including an RA-5C of RVAH-12, A-4C Skyhawks of VA-146, Grumman A-6A Intruders of VA-196, and F-4B Phantoms of VF-142 and VF-143. However, the stranger in their midst is the black-painted KA-3B Skywarrior belonging to a detachment of VAP-61 'World Recorders'. These aircraft were not part of the ship's regular air wing (CVW-14) but were deployed on board for a series of night interdiction attacks on Viet Cong truck convoys using infrared detection equipment. *USN*

Opposite below: An RA-5C Vigilante off RVAH-1 'Smokin' Tigers' landing aboard the USS *Saratoga* (CVA-60) in April 1969. The tail code AC was allocated to the ship's air wing (CVW-03), while in this view the raised fuselage profile behind the cockpit and the under-fuselage camera pack, features that distinguish this version of the Vigilante, are clearly visible. The ship only carried out one Vietnam deployment, between April 1972 and February 1973, as the war was ending and at that time RVAH-1 was still aboard. *USN*

A close-up view of some of CVW-3s aircraft ranged on the deck of the nuclear-powered USS *Enterprise* (CVAN-65) as she returns to her Californian home port of Alameda in June 1966 after her first Vietnam deployment. Most noticeable are the Skyhawks of VA-36 'Roadrunners' and VA-76 'Spirits' drawn up in a triangular formation, which was something of the ship's trademark on such occasions. Behind them are two RA-5C Vigilantes of RVAH-7 and a single AEW E-1B Tracer of Detachment M, VAW-11. *USN*

The USS *Enterprise* carried out a total of six Vietnam deployments, but the fourth one was marred by tragedy. On 14 January 1969, while carrying out pre-deployment exercises off Hawaii, a Mk.32 Zuni rocket loaded on an F-4J Phantom exploded when it became overheated by the hot exhaust from an adjacent auxiliary starter unit. The effect was catastrophic as fires spread across the flight deck, destroying fifteen aircraft, killing twenty-seven men and injuring 314 others. This image shows some of the effects of the fire as the crew carry out clearance operations. There are several burnt-out aircraft and at top left can be seen a large hole in the armoured flight deck. Despite the damage, the ship was repaired and ready for service less than two months later. *NMNA*

The presence of heavily armed aircraft on a crowded flight deck was always a dangerous set of circumstances and several carriers suffered serious fires similar to that experienced by the *Enterprise*. This is the earlier scene on 29 July 1967 aboard the USS *Forrestal* when, again, a Zuni rocket cooked off and hit a parked A-4C Skyhawk. This damage could have been contained, but some unstable 1,000lb bombs had been stowed on deck and these exploded in the heat of the resulting fire, causing substantial damage. A staggering 134 men were killed, another sixty-two injured, and twenty-one aircraft were destroyed. The ship had only just commenced her first Vietnam combat deployment but was then forced to withdraw, subsequent repairs not being completed until April 1968. *USN*

Apart from the dangers of operating from crowded flight decks, there was the additional hazard of enemy action. On 20 October, Lieutenant (j.g.) Denny Earl was flying an A-4E Skyhawk of VA-163 from the USS *Oriskany* (CV-34) when he was hit by AA fire over North Vietnam. A 0.5-in bullet shattered both his legs and left him in pain and bleeding profusely, despite which he continued on his mission, made an accurate bomb drop and set course back to the ship guided by his wingman. On advice from the ship's doctor, he inflated his G-suit, which acted as a tourniquet and helped stem the flow of blood. Despite being on the verge of fainting, he made a perfect approach and landing before running into the nylon emergency barrier, which had been erected to ensure that only the one approach would be needed. Thanks to prompt action by the ship's medical team, Denny later made a full recovery and continued his flying career. *NHHC*

Above: After a distinguished record in the Korean War, the piston-engined A-1 Skyraider was still in service, especially aboard the various Essex class carriers, during the opening stages of the Vietnam War. This A-1H single-seat attack variant belongs to VA-152 'Friendlies' aboard the USS *Oriskany* (CV-34) in 1966, during the ship's second Vietnam deployment. On the front line between June and November, VA-152 lost no fewer than four Skyraiders to enemy action; the pilot of one was recovered but the others were listed as either KIA or MIA. Attack versions of the Skyraider were finally withdrawn from front-line service in 1968, having been replaced by A-4 Skyhawks or A-6 Intruders. *NMNA*

Opposite above: Pilots of CVW-5 aboard the Essex class carrier USS *Bon Homme Richard* in March 1967 are briefed for their first attack mission over North Vietnam at the start of the ship's third Vietnam deployment, which proved to be a hectic affair with no shortage of action. During the period February to August 1967, the ship's fighter squadrons (VF-24 and VF-211 equipped with F-8 Crusaders) claimed eight MiG-17s destroyed, while an A-4C of VA-76 claimed another. However, some twenty-one US aircraft were lost to enemy action (9 Crusaders, 10 Skyhawks and 2 Skyraiders) and only eight pilots were recovered. The rest were either listed as KIA or MIA and others were taken prisoner, with some subsequently dying in captivity. *USN*

Opposite below: The USS *Bon Homme Richard* (CVA-31) was one of four Essex class carriers deployed off Vietnam in the CVA role having undergone the full SCB-125, which included the fitting of steam catapults as well as constructing a fully angled deck. This enabled them to operate jet aircraft such as the F-8 Crusader, A-4 Skyhawk and, on occasions, A-3 Skywarriors, although the larger and heavier F-4 Phantom II could not be accommodated. Noticeable in this view of the *Bon Homme Richard* in the Gulf of Tonkin in November 1964 is the array of radar antenna. To the left of the mainmast is the SPS-43 long-range air search radar while to the right is the circular array of the SPS-30 3D radar (i.e. with height finding capability). *NMNA*

Above: Prior to the Vietnam War, all three of the Midway class carriers had been modernised under the SCB-110 scheme in which the ships were rebuilt with an angled deck and fitted with steam catapults. This enabled them to operate F-4 Phantoms was well as other current jets. Of the three, the *Franklin D. Roosevelt* made only one Vietnam deployment while USS *Coral Sea* made no less than seven. The USS *Midway* made only three deployments, but between 1966 and 1970 was undergoing an extensive SCB-101 rebuild, which included an enlarged flight deck and new lifts. Here she is on her final deployment (April 1972 to February 1973), with a pair of VA-93 'Blue Blazers' A-7B Corsair IIs overhead. *NMNA*

Opposite above: The Vietnam War was officially brought to a close by the Paris Peace Accord, signed on 27 January 1973. Among the carriers on deployment at that point were the USS *America* (CVA-66) and USS *Ranger* (CVA-61), here cruising off Vietnam just before the former departed for her home port at Norfolk, Virginia. This photo usefully shows the main external difference between the Forrestal class (USS *Ranger*, background) and the succeeding Kitty Hawk class (USS *America*, foreground), which is the positioning of the starboard side deck-edge lifts. Those on the former are positioned one forward and two aft of the island superstructure, while this arrangement is reversed in the latter. *USN*

Opposite below: The various supercarriers (Forrestal and Kitty Hawk classes, plus the nuclear-powered *Enterprise*) made a total of thirty-one Vietnam deployments between 1964 and 1973. The one exception was the USS *John F. Kennedy* (CVA-67), which was commissioned later in 1968 and subsequently made several deployments with the US 6th Fleet in the Mediterranean and North Atlantic during the Vietnam era. Although much of the time was taken up with various NATO exercises, during the Mediterranean deployments there was a coup in Libya and unrest in the Lebanon, and then in late 1973 there was the Egypt-Israel Yom Kippur War. In all of these, the ship was in a heightened state of readiness, at times with fully armed aircraft on standby. In this 1969 photo, a pair of F-4B Phantoms of VF-14 'Tophatters' are readied on the catapults and parked behind are other Phantoms of VF-32 'Swordsmen'. In the foreground are RA-5C Vigilantes of RVAH-14 'Eagle Eyes'. *NHHC*

Above: Between deployments, the *John F. Kennedy* was often occupied in training for both her own air wing (CVW-I) and those of various shore-based Reserve units. This F-8H Crusader, which is just landing aboard in August 1971, is from Dallas-based VF-202 'Superheaters', which was part of Reserve Carrier Air Wing 20 (RCVW-20) and was carrying out routine carrier qualification training. The tail fin carries the AF code for RCVW-20, while the rudder is adorned with a representation of the Texas state flag, it being common practice for Reserve squadrons to show affiliation with their home state. *NHHC*

Opposite above: Although the F-4 Phantom II had its origins as an attack aircraft, it often ended up in dogfights with the North Vietnamese MiGs. However, its forte remained as an attack bomber and it was capable of carrying up to 16,000lb of ordnance. This is an F-4B belonging to VF154 aboard the USS *Ranger* (CVA-61) during the ship's third Vietnam deployment. On this mission, flown in February 1968, the squadron was supporting the 3rd US Marine Division, which was coming under fire from an NVA artillery position. *NARA*

Opposite below: In April 1975, the fall of Saigon was imminent and Operation Frequent Wind was put in place to evacuate US civilian staff and Vietnamese citizens deemed 'at risk'. To cover the evacuations four carriers were deployed – *Coral Sea*, *Enterprise*, *Midway* and *Hancock*. Over 50,000 people were evacuated by transport aircraft from Tan Son Nhat airport until 28 April, when it came under attack. Over the next two days, evacuation then centred on the US Embassy compound in Saigon, from which a total of 7,368 persons (US and Vietnamese) were flown out by helicopter to the carriers USS *Hancock* and USS *Midway* stationed offshore. This is the scene aboard the *Hancock*, where a pair of USMC CH-53D Sea Stallion helicopters have brought in a group of Vietnamese families whose numbers far exceed the nominal fifty-five-person cabin capacity of the CH-53D. *USN*

Chapter 5

Helicopters and ASW

By 1945, the means of detecting and attacking submarines had been refined to a high degree and incorporated the use of both land- and ship-based aircraft. However, in the post-war period, particularly from the early 1950s onwards, the Soviet submarine fleet grew both in numbers and in technical efficiency, and so anti-submarine warfare remained a high priority.

In terms of carrier-based ASW aircraft, the faithful TBM Avenger remained a useful asset but was eventually supplanted by another Grumman product, the AF Guardian. This was designed to work in pairs as a hunter-killer team, with one aircraft carrying the search radar and other detection equipment while the other carried the necessary weapons (depth charges, rockets, torpedoes) to make an attack. A logical progression was to produce a larger aircraft that could carry out both tasks but was still able to operate from the fleet's many Essex class carriers. The Grumman S2F Tracker, which entered service in 1954, fulfilled this role but required a considerable scale of support equipment aboard the parent carrier. Consequently, many of the Essex class, which were becoming redundant in the attack carrier role, were converted to act as specialist ASW carriers (designated CVS) although they usually embarked a squadron of A-4 Skyhawks for self-protection and to retain a limited attack capability. The ultimate carrier-based ASW aircraft was the jet-powered Lockheed S-3 Viking, which began to enter service just at the time of the final withdrawal from Vietnam in 1974/75. Since then it has proved surprisingly successful in other roles such as an aerial tanker, electronic intelligence gathering and even for attacking surface vessels using Harpoon anti-ship missiles.

The US Navy was quick to realise the potential of the helicopter and as early as 1942 acquired a Sikorsky YR-4B from the Army for trials. However, the early helicopters had only limited load-carrying abilities and although useful for roles such as SAR and casualty evacuation, they could not carry the weapons or equipment needed for ASW purposes. In the early 1950s, a version of the Sikorsky S-55 (HO4S) provided an interim solution, but it was not until the advent of the larger HSS-1 Seabat, followed by the very successful HSS-2/SH-3 Sea King in 1961, that the full potential of the helicopter in the ASW role could be realised. Subsequently, smaller ASW helicopters such as the Kaman SH-2 Seasprite were procured for deployment aboard surface warships other than aircraft carriers. By the 1990s, both the Sea King and the Seasprite had been replaced by adapted versions of the SH-60 Seahawk.

Experience during the Second World War demonstrated the vital role that long-range maritime patrol aircraft could play in combatting the submarine menace. For most of that period, the US Navy preferred to use flying boats and amphibians, particularly in the Pacific, where there were few airfields that could accommodate large aircraft, and they continued to be used as late as the mid-1960s. In the period covered by this book, the Navy deployed a series of increasingly sophisticated land-based maritime patrol aircraft capable of carrying out the ASW mission across the wide expanses of the world's oceans — a mission that had the highest priority when the potential enemy was the ballistic missile-armed, nuclear-powered submarine.

The anti-submarine TBM-3E Avenger carried an APS-4 radar in a pod under the starboard wing and was armed with rockets, depth bombs or homing torpedoes. Most of those in service after the war were modernised as the TBM-3E2 and could be identified by an external arrester hook under the tail, which replaced the original faired-in 'stinger' hook. That feature can be seen on this pair flown by VC-23, which was deployed aboard the USS *Bairoko* (CVE-115) operating in support of operations off Korea in 1950–1. Subsequently, a more specialised version was produced as the TBM-3S, which had all gun armament removed and a searchlight added under the port wing. *NMNA*

Above: Following the end of the Second World War, the US Navy possessed dozens of escort carriers, most of which were sold off or placed in reserve. However, several of the Commencement Bay class were recommissioned after the outbreak of the Korean War and were adapted for use as ASW carriers. This is USS *Point Cruz* (CVE-119) off the coast of Japan in July 1953. On board are TBM-3W and TBM-3S Avengers of VS-23 together with a single Sikorsky HO4S helicopter belonging to a detachment of HS-2. *NHHC*

Opposite above: Beginning in 1950, the ASW Avengers were gradually replaced by the Grumman AF Guardian. Conceived as a replacement for the Avenger in the torpedo bomber role under the designation TB3F, it was later classified as an attack bomber, hence the AF designation. A tail-mounted jet engine supplemented a nose-mounted R-2800 Double Wasp radial engine and the prototype XTB3F-1 flew on 19 December 1945. However, the jet engine proved of limited value and was later removed while the aircraft was redesigned for the ASW role. As such, it was produced in two forms, the radar-equipped AF-2W and the AF-2S weapon carrier, which together operated as a hunter-killer team. This pair of Guardians are flown by VS-24, which was the first to receive the new aircraft, in September 1951. *NARA*

Opposite below: The Grumman AF-2W variant was easily distinguished by the large ventral radome housing the antenna of the AN/APS-20 radar (which was also carried by the earlier TBM-3W Avengers – see Chapter 6). It also carried ESM equipment in the form of an AN/APR-98 receiver to detect and monitor radio and other electronic emissions and an AN/AP-70 direction finder to help pinpoint the source of such emissions. To operate the radar and other electronic equipment the AF-2W carried two extra crew in addition to the normal pilot and navigator, and these were accommodated within the fuselage compartment. *NARA*

Above: A ground view of the AF-2S strike variant. The pod under the starboard wing houses a short-range AN/APS-30 radar while under the other wing is a similarly sized pod housing a powerful searchlight. Up to 4,000lb of torpedoes, bombs or depth charges could be carried in the under-fuselage bomb bay, and there was provision for up to six HVAR on underwing racks. This was twice the amount of ordnance that the Avenger could carry and the Guardian's range was 50 per cent greater. However, it suffered from a high accident rate and was rapidly phased out of service after the Korean War, the last front-line squadron relinquishing its Guardians in August 1955. *NARA*

Opposite above: As early as 1949, the US Navy recognised the limitations of the two-aircraft hunter-killer team and invited development of a larger aircraft that could combine both functions in a single airframe. The outcome was the Grumman S2F Tracker (redesigned S-2 after 1962), which first flew on 4 December 1952. It was powered by two 1,525hp R-1820 radial engines and a capacious fuselage accommodated four crew and a range of electronic equipment. This included an APS-38 radar in a retractable under-fuselage dome, ECM receiver and direction finder, and an MAD sensor on a tail boom. The lowered radome and extended MAD boom are shown by this early production S2F-1 Tracker. *NARA*

Opposite below: The S2F-1 Tracker began to reach operational squadrons from February 1954 onwards and rapidly became the US Navy's primary carrier-based ASW aircraft. In addition to a 4,800lb weapon load, the Tracker also carried thirty-two sonobuoys housed in the rear of the engine nacelles. This S2F-1 is flown by VS-30, which had received its first examples in October 1954 and subsequently served aboard carriers in the Atlantic and Mediterranean. In 1960, it became land based at NAS Key West as part of RCVG-50 (Replacement Carrier Antisubmarine Warfare Air Group 50) and was tasked with training new crews to operate the Tracker. Note the underwing rocket load and the searchlight pod under the starboard wing. *NMNA*

Increasingly, the carrier air groups were composed of jet aircraft, and separate stowage arrangements had been made for the Avgas required by the piston-engined Tracker. Also, anti-submarine patrols could last for several hours, which made it difficult to fit in with the carrier's flight deck operating cycle. In the 1950s there were no airborne digital computers to process the data that was received from the sonobuoys and other sensors, so this instead was transmitted to the parent carrier on which the requisite command and control facilities had to be accommodated. To overcome these issues many of the Essex class carriers were refitted as ASW carriers (CVS), including the USS *Randolph* (CVS-15), shown here underway in 1959 immediately following her conversion. On deck are the S2F-1 Trackers of VS-36 'Gray Wolves'. *USN*

The US Navy had taken an early interest in the use of helicopters and by the time of the Korean War, most carriers embarked a Sikorsky HO3S (S-51) for plane guard and rescue missions. However, it was too small to carry equipment or weapons for ASW purposes and it was not until the larger HO4S (Sikorsky S-55) became available in the early 1950s that this became feasible. These HSO4-3 helicopters belong to HS-4 'Black Knights', which was the first ASW squadron to deploy aboard an aircraft carrier, in this case the escort carrier USS *Badoeng Strait* (CVE-116) in July 1954. However, in practice, the HO4S proved unsuitable for the ASW task due to its relatively short endurance and limited load capacity, although if not armed it could carry an AN/AQS-1 dipping sonar. *NHHC*

Some of the issues identified with the HO4S were addressed in its successor, the larger Sikorsky HSS-1 Seabat, although again they were configured to act either as hunters or killers. In the former role, an improved AN/AQWS-4 sonar was installed while the armed version could carry a pair of lightweight Mk.43 or Mk.44 homing torpedoes. The Seabat equipped several US Navy squadrons, which were usually deployed aboard the converted Essex class ASW carriers. This example belongs to HS-9 'Sea Griffins' and is shown in July 1959 landing aboard the USS *Randolph* (CVS-15), which had just recommissioned as an ASW carrier. *NMNA*

Perhaps the most fearsome ASW weapon available to the US Navy in the late 1950s/early 1960s was the Mk.101 (Lulu) nuclear depth charge, which was fitted with an 11-kiloton yield W34 warhead. From an operational point of view, its main advantage was that it didn't need to be dropped with any great degree of accuracy; its detonation would destroy any submarine in the near vicinity. On the other hand, there were numerous problems associated with its storage and handling, and there was always the potential of collateral damage to adjacent friendly forces. A Mk.101 depth charge is here loaded on an HSS-1 Seabat for publicity purposes, but it was too heavy (1,200lb) for practical operational deployment by these helicopters. *USN*

Above: In a process paralleling the evolution of fixed-wing ASW aircraft, in 1957 the US Navy called for a helicopter that could combine the hunter-killer roles in a single airframe. The outcome was the Sikorsky HSS-2 Sea King (designated SH-3 after 1962), which was powered by a pair of General Electric T58 turboshaft engines and equipped with an AQS-10 (later AQS-13) dipping sonar. In addition, it could carry an 840lb weapon load including torpedoes and/or depth charges. First flown in March 1959, it entered service in September 1961, initially with HS-3 and HS10, but subsequently with virtually all of the Navy's ASW helicopter squadrons. This SH-3A deploying of the sensor for the AQS-13 sonar belongs to VC-2 'Golden Falcons', part of CVSG-57 aboard the USS *Hornet* (CVS-12) in 1962. *NMNA*

Opposite above: The Sea King was destined to have a long and distinguished career with the US Navy and was only withdrawn from front-line service in the 1990s, but transport and utility versions continued to equip Reserve units until the last was retired in 2006. It was widely exported to overseas air arms and even today, a few remain in service. This SH-3A Sea King was one of a batch that re-equipped HS-1 'Seahorses' in 1962, the squadron having previously flown the HSS-1 Seabat. This photo was taken in the 1960s, when the HS-1 was a Fleet Replacement Squadron based at NAS Key West to train ground and air crews to operate the Sea King. *USN*

Opposite below: The Kaman H-2 Seasprite was initially ordered as a utility and SAR helicopter for the US Navy. However, in 1970, the Navy ordered a modified version (the SH-2D) to act as a Light Airborne Multi-Purpose System (LAMPS) helicopter to operate from destroyers and other surface vessels apart from aircraft carriers. LAMPS included ASW systems and the SH-2D could carry two Mk.46 homing torpedoes. The improved SH-2F entered service in 1971, and one is shown aboard the guided missile cruiser USS *Wainwright* (CG-28) in 1988. It is flown by Light Helicopter Anti-Submarine Squadron HSL-32, which operated Seasprites from 1973 until 1994, when it was disestablished. *US Defense Imagery*

The Seasprite was regarded as an interim type and the Navy required a larger helicopter that could carry the more advanced LAMPS Mk.III equipment. To reduce cost, the Navy looked at existing airframes and selected the US Army's UH-60 Blackhawk. This resulted in the SH-60B Seahawk, which entered service in 1984, replacing the Seasprite aboard destroyers, frigates and other warships. Subsequently, the SH-60F Seahawk was a further development intended as a Sea King replacement aboard the carriers. The LAMPS III equipment was replaced by an AQS-13F dipping sonar, which was supplemented by the APS-124 radar and a towed MAD array. A full outfit of sonobuoys is carried as well as up to three lightweight homing torpedoes. The SH-60F was first deployed in 1991, and this example flown by HS-3 'Tridents' is just landing aboard the USS *Theodore Roosevelt* (CVN-71) in early 2003. *USN*

The replacement for the long-serving piston-engined S-2 Tracker was the much more sophisticated jet-powered S-3A Viking, which first entered service with VS-41, an ASW training squadron, in 1974, with operational deployments following in 1975. The S-3A carried a full range of ASW sensors including a FLIR sensor, ASQ-81 MAD on a retractable boom, APS-116 high-resolution radar, and an acoustic processing system to collate data obtained from sonobuoys (sixty carried). An internal bomb bay can accommodate four torpedoes or equivalent ordnance, and underwing hard points can carry various bombs, rockets or missiles. Landing aboard the USS *Kitty Hawk* (CV-63) in April 1983 is an S-3A of VS-29 'Dragonflies'. *NARA*

With the advent of the S-3B version in 1988, the Viking effectively became a multi-role aircraft. The ASW avionics were upgraded and an APS-137 ISAR (Inverse Synthetic Aperture Radar) added as well as new ESM equipment and chaff/flare dispensers. Provision was made for the carriage of a pair of Harpoon anti-ship missiles which gave the Viking an ASUW capability, while the ISAR and other monitoring equipment meant that it could carry out ISR missions. This pair of S-3B Vikings from VC-31 'Topcats' is pictured over the carrier USS *John F. Kennedy* (CV-67) in March 2002. Note that aircraft 706 has a 'buddy' inflight refuelling pack under its port wing and in this manner the versatile Vikings were often used as tankers for other aircraft in the carrier's air wing. *USN*

One of the most important wartime flying boats was the Martin PBM Mariner, which entered service in 1941. The final variant was the PBM-5, which remained in production until 1949 and was used by US patrol squadrons until the last was retired in 1956. This PBM-5, operated by VP-47 'The Golden Swordsmen', is ashore on beaching gear at NAS Kaneohe Bay in 1949, shortly before the squadron relocated to Alameda, California. *NMNA*

The prototype Martin XP5M-1 Marlin, which was based on the previous PBM Mariner, first flew on 30 May 1948. In production P5M-1s, the nose turret was replaced by a large radome for an APS-80 search radar (requiring a raised flight deck) and 3,350hp Wright R-3350 engines were mounted in extended nacelles, the rear sections of which incorporated bomb bays. Marlins entered service (with VP-44) in April 1952, and this formation, photographed in 1954, is flown by VP-56 'Dragons' and illustrates the initial P5M-1 with a low-set tailplane. Most of the early Marlins were fitted with an extensive array of ASW equipment and as such were designated P5M-1S. *NMNA*

Above: The redesigned P5M-2 was produced in 1953 and entered service the following year. The major external change was the adoption of a prominent T-tail and the deletion of the rear gun turret. In all, a total of 259 Marlin variants were delivered before production ended in 1960, many of which were fitted with specialised ASW equipment as the P5M-1S or P5M-2S (SP-5A and SP-5B after 1962). This photo shows an SP-5B of VP-49 taking off in 1963, and the last Marlin operational squadron was VP-40, which was only stood down as late as 1967 after being tasked with surveillance over the Mekong Delta during the Vietnam War. *NMNA*

Opposite above: In 1942, the US Navy began to obtain examples of the USAAF's B-24 Liberator for use as a long-range maritime patrol aircraft, designated PB4Y-1 in Navy service. In 1944, a new version was developed specifically to Navy requirements as the PB4Y-2 Privateer, with a tall single tail fin replacing the twin tail configuration of the original Liberator. Many Privateers were adapted for ASW missions with an APS-15 radar as the PB4Y-2S, including this one from VP-23 'Seahawks', which flew the Privateer from 1946 to 1953, although between 1946 and 1949, it flew PB4Y-2Ms on weather and hurricane surveillance missions before converting to the ASW role with PB4M-2S Privateers in 1949. The last US Navy PB4Y-2s were retired in 1954. *NMNA*

Opposite below: The Lockheed P2V Neptune was to be the main equipment for US Navy patrol squadrons from 1947 until well into the 1960s. The prototype XP2V-1 flew on 17 May 1945 and the first production Neptunes began to reach operational squadrons in 1947. In the meantime, a modified P2V-1 named 'Truculent Turtle' established a world distance record of 11,236 miles in September 1946, flying from Perth, Australia, to Columbus, Ohio, in the USA. The P2V-2 was an improved version and this example had been delivered to VP-861 (a Reserve squadron) in September 1950. By the time this photo was taken in 1953, the squadron had been redesignated as VP-18 'Flying Phantoms', which continued to operate various versions of the Neptune until disestablished in 1968. *NARA*

Above: The ultimate production version of the Neptune was the P2V-7 (SP-2H), which was first flown in April 1954. To boost performance a pair of underwing pod-mounted 3,400lb.s.t. J34 turbojets were fitted as standard following experience with a batch of similarly modified P2V-5s (ultimately, almost all P2V-5s received the jets and were designated as P2V-5F/SP-2E). ASW equipment installed in both variants included the prominent tail-mounted MAD gear, an APS/AN-20 search radar and Jezebel/Julie systems for monitoring active/passive sonobuoys. This SP-2H belongs to VP-7 'Black Falcons' based at NAS Jacksonville, Florida, which flew them from 1962 until disestablished in 1969. *USN*

Opposite above: The P2V-7 and modified P2V-5 Neptunes served as the standard US Navy maritime patrol aircraft until the mid-1960s (in 1964, no less than nineteen squadrons were equipped with Neptunes) while some Reserve squadrons only retired their last examples in 1978. Its replacement was the turboprop P-3A Orion, which was an adaption of the Lockheed Electra airliner, and an early production example is shown in 1963 alongside a P-2H Neptune, which it was in the process of replacing. The first operational squadron to receive the Orion was VP-8 based at NAS Patuxent River, and by 1967, the P-3A had re-equipped fourteen Neptune squadrons and SP-5B Marlin flying boats in five squadrons. ASW equipment included a nose-mounted APS/AN-80 search radar, ASQ-10 MAD gear and an ASR-3 diesel exhaust detector. *NMNA*

Opposite below: Since its entry into service, the Orion was progressively upgraded and the final production version was the P-3C. Improved and additional ASW equipment was fitted, and this has been the subject of further upgrades throughout the aircraft's service life. An internal bomb bay and up to ten underwing hard points can carry a maximum 20,000lb weapon load, which can include Harpoon anti-ship missiles as well as a range of torpedoes, bombs and rockets. A total of 757 Orions of all versions were produced up to 1990. Shown just after taking off from NAS North Island, California, is a P-3C Orion of VP-40 'Fighting Marlins', the squadron's nickname being a reference to the fact that it had flown Marlin flying boats before converting to Orions in 1967. *USN*

Chapter 6

AEW and Electronic Warfare

In the closing stages of the Pacific War, a need arose to provide carrier task forces with an earlier warning of attacks than that provided by shipboard radars. In response, Project Cadillac was initiated in 1943, and this resulted in a new radar, AN/APS-20, which could detect targets at up to 100 miles range and was small enough to be housed in a carrier-based aircraft, initially the Grumman TBM-3W Avenger. By the time of the Korean War in 1950, every carrier embarked a detachment of AEW aircraft, although by then the Avenger had been replaced by more capable versions of the Douglas AD Skyraider. Also by that time, many Skyraiders were adapted to engage in the increasingly important field of electronic warfare (EW). This involved the passive role of monitoring and cataloguing enemy radio and radar emissions as well as the more active tasks of jamming, disrupting and confusing the sources of such emissions. The increasing quantity and sophistication of the equipment needed for these missions resulted in the conversion of larger aircraft such as the Douglas A3D Skywarrior for the EW role as well as the production of specialised versions of attack aircraft such as the A-6 Intruder. This resulted in the EA-6B Prowler, which was still in service at the time of the Gulf War in 2003.

Although AEW versions of the Skyraider gave sterling service for many years, the AN/APS-20 lacked the performance required as the need for earlier threat detection at longer ranges arose with the appearance of missile-armed jet bombers. The twin-engined Grumman Tracker had entered service in 1954 and had provided the basis for the Trader COD transport, which featured an increased volume fuselage. This airframe proved capable of carrying the rotating antenna of an APS-82 radar in a large aerodynamic radome mounted above the fuselage, and accommodating two radar operators and their equipment as well as the two flight crew. The result was the WF-1/ E-1 Tracer, which provided vital AEW support for the fleet until replaced by the more advanced turboprop-powered E-2 Hawkeye, which entered service in 1964 (the improved E-2D remains in service today).

In addition to carrier-based AEW aircraft, the Navy also acquired AEW versions of Lockheed's L1049 Super Constellation airliner. Entering service as the WV-2 (later EC-121K) Warning Star in 1954, these aircraft were primarily deployed as part of US air defences, a duty shared with the USAF, in barrier forces off the east and west coasts of the continental United Sates. Subsequently, many of the Navy EC-121Ks were transferred to the USAF, who took over the whole air defence network and later replaced the Warning Stars with the Boeing E-3 Sentry (an adaptation of the Boeing 707 airliner). However, the Navy retained some EC-121s, which were deployed off Vietnam and were also used for other tasks such as weather reconnaissance and EW missions before being replaced by P-3 Orions.

The most suitable aircraft to carry the APS-20 radar was the Grumman TBM Avenger which, when fitted with the new radar and a rotating antenna in a bulbous under-fuselage housing, was designated as the TBM-3W. The rear gun turret was removed and the after cockpit faired over to enclose a space for two radar operators. The latter's function was to monitor the technical operation of the radar whose signals were relayed to operators on a ship who would then direct the fighters. Following successful trials, the system was on the verge of operational deployment when the war ended in August 1945. *NARA*

By the time of the Korean War, the TBM-3W had been replaced by AEW versions of the Douglas AD Skyraider. This formation of AD-4Ws belong to Detachment 35 of VC-12, which was deployed as part of CVG-6 aboard the USS *Midway* (CVA-41) from 1951 to 1954. The original service version was the AD-3W, but the AD-4W was produced in greater numbers and was powered by an improved version of the Wright R-3350 engine. The radar was the same APS-20 as used by the previous Avenger but in the Skyraider the two operators were accommodated in an enclosed cabin faired in behind the pilot's cockpit. *NMNA*

The AD-5 (A-IE) was a two-seat version of the Skyraider in which the crew sat side by side in a widened forward fuselage. First flown in August 1951, it was intended for the attack mission but proved adaptable to many other roles. A four-seat night attack version was the AD-5N (A-1G), and the AD-5W (A-IE) was produced as the AEW version, also with a crew of four. Fifty-four AD-4Ns were later modified to act as ECM aircraft, redesignated as the AD-5Q (EA-1F), and in 1966, six EA-1Es were also converted to the EA-1F configuration. Electronic equipment included an APS-31 ground-mapping radar and provision for an APS-19 radar for intercepting airborne targets, as well as pods carrying jamming equipment and chaff dispensers. This formation is flown by AD-5Qs of VAW-33 'Night Hawks', part of CVG-7, which served aboard the USS *Independence* (CVA-62) from August 1960 to August 1962. *USN*

Several other front-line aircraft were used in the EW role, one of the most notable being the A3D-2Q (EA-3B), which was adapted from the Douglas Skywarrior nuclear bomber and played an important role in Vietnam operations. A pressurised crew compartment replaced the bomb bay and this accommodated three ECM operators and a tactical co-ordinator, with the normal three crew (pilot, second pilot/navigator, ECM operator) occupying the forward cockpit. A comprehensive range of electronic equipment was installed, much of it in a ventral 'canoe' fairing, and a prominent in-flight refuelling probe was fitted on the port side of the forward fuselage. Several of these features can be seen on this EA-3B of VQ-2 'Batmen' doing a bolter after missing the wires aboard the USS *Saratoga* (CV-60) in March 1986. *US Defense Imagery*

The Grumman EA-6B Prowler was based on the A-6A all-weather attack aircraft, which had entered service in 1963, and an EW version (EA-6A) for the USMC followed in 1965. However, this was a two-crew aircraft (pilot and ECM operator) and it was soon realised that the increasingly sophisticated equipment carried could not be monitored and operated by one ECMO. Consequently, a stretched four-seat version, the EA-6B, was developed, which was first deployed to Vietnam aboard the USS *America* (CVA-66) in June 1972. This overhead view of an EA-6B Prowler clearly shows the lengthened forward fuselage and the position of the four crew members. *USN*

Above: A total of 170 Prowlers were produced between 1970 and 1971, in addition to several prototypes and development aircraft. Its primary function was to support air and ground operations by identifying and suppressing enemy electronic equipment (communications, radars, guidance systems etc.). To do this the aircraft carried up to five jammer pods and/or chaff dispensers, a nose-mounted surveillance radar, and self-protection countermeasure systems. It could also gather electronic signals intelligence (SIGINT), and the Prowler's equipment has been constantly upgraded, such as using more powerful digital computers to automate some of the tasks. Upgrade ICAP II introduced the facility to carry HARM anti-radar missiles. These EA-6Bs aboard the USS *Kitty Hawk* (CV-63) in 1983 belong to VAQ-129 'Vikings', which became the Fleet Replacement Squadron for the Prowler in 1970. *USN*

Opposite above: A requirement for a land-based, long-range AEW aircraft in 1945 was met by the conversion of surplus ex-USAAF B-17G Fortress bombers, which were stripped of most of their armament and fitted with an AN/APS-20 radar with its antenna in an under-fuselage dome. Painted in the then standard midnight blue, the thirty-one conversions were designated PB-1W, some of which remained in service until the mid-1950s. The one shown here was one of several allocated to VX-4 in 1946 to develop equipment and procedures for the AEW task. *USN*

Opposite below: Apart from Lockheed Constellation transports (R7O-1 and R7V-1, C-121 after 1962), in 1949 the Navy also obtained two Model L749 Constellations (redesignated PO-1W or WV-1) fitted with an APS-20 search radar with a ventral-mounted antenna and an APS-45 height finder in a prominent dorsal radome. Following successful trials, orders were placed for the definitive WV-2 Warning Star (EC-121K from 1962) based on the L1049 Super Constellation, and these began to enter service in 1954. Their main task, in conjunction with USAF EC-121s, was to provide radar 'barrier' zones off the coast of the continental USA to give early warning of potential bomber or missile attacks. This EC-121K was photographed at NAS Barbers Point, Hawaii, in 1965, just before the Pacific barrier force (BARPAC) was stood down in September of that year. However, other EC-121s provided AEW cover for naval operations during the Vietnam War and weather reconnaissance WC-131s were active until 1975. *NMNA*

Above: The Grumman TF-1/C-1A Trader was a derivative of the S2F Tracker (*see* Chapter 5), in which the fuselage volume was increased in order to accommodate cargo or up to nine passengers, and entered service in 1956. Four Traders were converted as the TF-1Q/EC-1A Electric Trader for the ECM role carrying monitoring receivers and jamming systems in underwing pods. They were delivered in 1957, but later, with the advent of the WF-2 Tracer (*see* below) in the 1960s, the electronic equipment was removed and they reverted to a utility/transport role. The two EC-1As shown were flown by a detachment of VAW-33 'Night Hawks' aboard the USS *Wasp* (CVA-18) in late 1961, although the squadron's main equipment was the AD-5W Skyraider. *USN*

Opposite above: A more successful derivative of the Tracker was an AEW version with a large radome above the fuselage, which would house the antenna for the AN/APS-82 radar. Designated WF-1, it was initially based on the airframe of the ASW Tracker, but it was subsequently realised that the larger cabin of the TF-1 Trader offered more space for the radar equipment and its operators. This became the WF-2 (later E-1B) Tracer, which first flew in March 1958 and entered service (with VAW-12) in January 1960. Because of the radome, the wings utilised Grumman's patented 'Sto-wing' arrangement to fold alongside the fuselage, as demonstrated by this E-1B preparing to depart from the USS *Hancock* (CVA-19) in August 1962. *USN*

Opposite below: These two WF-2 Tracers are flown by VAW-11 'Early Elevens', one of the first squadrons involved in developing AEW techniques when it was formed in 1948 and subsequently converted to the WF-2 Tracer in 1959/60. As shown here, they were operating as part of CVG-19 aboard the Essex class carrier USS *Bon Homme Richard* (CVA-31) in 1961. The Tracer was used extensively in Vietnam, particularly in the earlier years of the war, but all were withdrawn by 1973 apart from four E-1Bs of RVAW-110, which made the type's final deployment aboard the carrier USS *Franklin D. Roosevelt* between November 1976 and April 1977. *NHHC*

121

The Grumman E-1 Tracer was always intended as an interim aircraft pending the development of a more capable platform. Grumman proposed their Design 123, which would carry a crew of five and featured a pylon-mounted revolving 'rotodome'. Power was provided by a pair of Allison T-56 turboprops, which would enable the aircraft to remain on station for up to six hours at an altitude of 25,000 feet. Initially designated W2F-1 (E-2A after 1962) and named Hawkeye, an aerodynamic prototype flew in October 1960. In January 1964, Hawkeyes began to replace the Tracers of VAW-11 based in California. The squadron was responsible for providing AEW detachments to carriers of the Pacific Fleet while VAW-12 provided similar service from its East Coast base (NAS Norfolk) to Atlantic Fleet carriers. By the time the Hawkeye was in service, the Vietnam War was intensifying and the type's first deployment to the Gulf of Tonkin was with Detachment C of VAW-11 aboard the USS *Kitty Hawk* (CVA-63) in October 1966. One of their E-2As is here being launched by one of the ship's steam catapults. *USN*

Experience in Vietnam showed that the E-2A Hawkeye was greatly superior to its predecessor, but eventually, most of the E-2As were modified to E-2B standard with improved computer facilities. The modified aircraft entered service from 1970, but an even more advanced variant, the E-2C, became operational in 1973, and by 1986 had replaced all earlier versions in both front-line and Reserve squadrons. It was initially equipped with a new AN/APS-120 radar, an AN/ALR-059 Passive Detection System, and other improved electronic equipment, but all of these systems were further upgraded or replaced over the next two decades. This E-2C Hawkeye of VAW-117 'Wallbangers' is preparing to depart from the USS *Nimitz* (CVN-68) in 2003. *USN*

The E-2C Hawkeye is normally operated by a crew of five. The flight deck crew comprise a pilot and co-pilot while in the rear cabin are a radar operator, an air controller and a combat information centre officer, all seated facing to port. The cabin is pressurised so that oxygen masks do not need to be worn – an important detail for flights that could last for up to six hours. At the front of the cabin is the radar operator (shown here), at the rear is the air controller and in the centre is the combat information centre officer, who also acts as the mission commander. Each has access to a multi-function Advanced Control Indicator Set (ACIS) built into a Q-70 display system, which can be programmed according to the operator's task. *USN*

Chapter 7

Taming the Bear
1975-1990

By the end of the fighting in Vietnam in September 1973, the US Navy had fourteen operational carriers in commission, of which there were only two Essex class (USS *Hancock*, USS *Oriskany*). The other Essex class carriers were being retired and many of the newer ships desperately needed refitting and updating after the strenuous pace of operations during the Vietnam War. In terms of aircraft, in July 1964 there were 3,552 front-line combat aircraft, and this had fallen to 2,961 (of which 1,822 were allocated to active Navy and Marine squadrons) by September 1975. In fact, the situation regarding aircraft was not as bad as the figures might have suggested as the quality and performance of the latest types offered a substantial improvement over those that they replaced. In particular, the new F-14 Tomcat, which had its initial combat debut in the last stages of the war, and the F-18 Hornet, which followed in the early 1980s, offered a substantial improvement over the F-4 Phantom II, which they gradually replaced. In the attack role, the piston-engined Skyraider and the small A-4 Skyhawk had been retired and replaced by A-6 Intruders and A-7 Corsair IIs, the latter performing extremely well in Vietnam, where it experienced one of the lowest combat loss rates despite the fact that it was employed almost exclusively on dangerous low-level attack missions. As a result of war experience, US naval aviation was extremely capable in the increasingly important roles of electronic warfare and AEW command and control systems, and this showed in the upgrades and improvements made to the EA-6 Growlers and E-2C Hawkeyes.

The retirement of the Essex class carriers included several that had been converted as anti-submarine carriers (CVS), and consequently, an ASW element was now included in the composition of the Carrier Air Wings (CVW) allocated to the carriers. This included S-3 Viking and Sea King (later also Seahawk) helicopters. As there was now no specialist ASW carrier (CVS), it was not necessary to designate others as attack carriers (CVA) and as a result, after 1975 all carriers were just classified as CV (or CVN) to indicate a spread of operational capabilities.

In a major boost to the Navy, the first of eventually ten Nimitz class nuclear-powered carriers was commissioned in 1975, although the programme spanned several decades and the last was not completed until 2009. These new carriers and aircraft gradually became the key components of US Navy strength. In many respects just in time, as from the mid-1970s, the Soviet Navy, under the leadership of Admiral Gorshkov, set out to become a true 'Blue Water' navy with the ability to challenge the US Navy whenever necessary. As well as four Kiev class hybrid aircraft carriers, their cruisers and destroyers were all equipped with long-range anti-ship missiles intended to strike at the US carriers. These were backed up by long-range missile-equipped bombers, which posed a significant threat, making the defence of carrier task forces a complex task involving fighters, missiles and airborne command and control assets. In answer to this threat, the Reagan administration authorised the concept of an expanded 600-ship navy, which the Soviets were hard-pressed to match. In fact, the financial strain of the naval power struggle was one of the factors that led to the apparent end of the Cold War in 1989 and the break-up of the Soviet Union in 1991.

Opposite: By 1976, the last of the long-serving Essex class had been decommissioned (except for USS *Lexington*, which continued as a training carrier until 1991) and the Midway class USS *Franklin D. Roosevelt* was also decommissioned in 1977, although her two sister ships served until the start of the 1990s. To set against these reductions, the USS *Nimitz* (CVAN-68) commissioned on 1 May 1975, the first of an eventual class of ten nuclear-powered carriers. She was initially laid down by the Newport News Shipbuilding and Dry Dock Co. in Newport News, Virginia, on 22 June 1968, and subsequently launched on 13 May 1972. In this view of the ship under construction, a prominent feature is the troughs to accommodate the four C-13 steam catapults. *USN*

After initial sea trials and commissioning, the *Nimitz* embarked Carrier Air Wing 8 (CVW-8) and in July and August 1975, she underwent her initial operational evaluation in the Guantánamo Bay Operating Area, Cuba, where she is shown taking on ordnance supplies from the ammunition ship USS *Mount Baker* (AE-34). The flight deck layout closely corresponded with that of the USS *John F. Kennedy* (CVA-67), with three lifts on the starboard side and one aft on the port side, sited clear of the angle deck runway. Aircraft ranged on deck include F-4J Phantom IIs, A-6E Intruders, EA-6B Prowlers, A-7E Corsair IIs, RA-5C Vigilantes, E-2B Hawkeyes and SH-3H Sea King helicopters. *NHHC*

Above: The conventionally powered USS *Kitty Hawk* (CV-63) underway in the Pacific in March 1978, with CVW-11 embarked. This was the ship's first deployment following a refit in which her aviation facilities were modified and improved to allow operation of two new aircraft types (F-14 Tomcat fighter and S-3 Viking ASW aircraft) while the defensive armament now comprised Sea Sparrow point-defence missiles instead of the previous medium-ranged RIM-2 Terrier. In this view, the F-14A Tomcats of VF-114 'Aardvarks' and VF-213 'Black Lions' are ranged aft. *NARA*

Opposite above: The Grumman F-14 Tomcat had stemmed from efforts begun in 1961 to combine the roles of the USAF's projected TFX tactical fighter with the US Navy's requirement for a Fleet Air Defence (FAD) fighter in a common airframe. This evolved into the F-111A, which was produced in large numbers for the Air Force, but only seven examples of the Navy's F-111B (shown here) were produced. First flown in May 1965, it was severely overweight and underpowered, and lacked the manoeuvrability to match that of the F-4 Phantom II, which it was intended to replace. The programme was cancelled in 1968, leaving the Navy free to develop an aircraft more suited to its particular requirements. *NMNA*

Opposite below: Following the cancellation of the F-111B, the Navy developed the Grumman F-14 Tomcat to meet the requirement for a Fleet Air Defence fighter that would be able to engage hostile aircraft long before they were in a position to launch anti-ship missiles. This was achieved by combining the powerful AN/AWG-9 track-while-scan radar with the long-range AIM-54 Phoenix air-to-air missile. The first pre-production YF-14A flew on 21 December 1970 but was lost in an accident on its second flight. However, the availability of other pre-production aircraft meant that the development programme was not significantly delayed and by September 1974, two Tomcat squadrons (VF-1, VF-2) were first deployed as part of CVW-14 aboard the USS *Enterprise* (CVAN-65) in time to cover the final withdrawal from Saigon in April 1975. This F-14A is a VF-2 'Bounty Hunters' aircraft being launched from the *Enterprise* on 28 April 1975. *NMNA*

Above: The F-14 can carry up to six AIM-54 Phoenix missiles paired with an AWG-9 fire-control system using a pulse-Doppler radar able to track up to twenty-four targets simultaneously at ranges of up to 240km (130nm). Development of the Phoenix began in late 1960 when Hughes started to evolve a new long-range missile, designated AAN-N-11 (later AIM-54A) by the Navy, together with the AN/AWG-9 FCS (fire-control system). This combination was originally intended as the main armament for the abortive F-111B. Flight tests of Phoenix prototypes began in 1965, and the AIM-54 and AN/AWG-9 were subsequently incorporated into the new F-14 Tomcat. Production missiles were delivered in 1973, ready for deployment with the first F-14A squadron in 1974. *US Defense Imagery*

Opposite above: The Soviet Tupolev Tu-16 (Badger) jet bomber had first flown as early as 1952 and was built in large numbers, including many specifically modified for the anti-shipping role and/or for maritime and ELINT reconnaissance missions. Carrying a pair of missiles such as the AS-6 Kingfish, which could be launched at a range of 200–300 miles, they posed a significant threat to the US carriers, especially if an attack was made by a large formation. It was to counter this scenario that the F-14 Tomcat and its long-range Phoenix missile was developed. This Badger-C is overflying the USS *Ranger* (CV-61) on a reconnaissance mission – a common occurrence during the 1980s. *USN*

Opposite below: Another Soviet aircraft commonly encountered over the world's oceans was the Tu-95 Bear, a unique turboprop-powered heavy bomber adapted for the maritime reconnaissance role. As well as gathering information and intelligence, the Bears could provide targeting information for anti-ship missiles launched from other platforms such as surface vessels and submarines. As such, they were always regarded as a potential threat and were regularly intercepted and monitored. On this occasion, an F-14A Tomcat from VF-11 'Red Rippers' has launched from the USS *John F. Kennedy* (CV-67) to intercept and escort a Tu-95D Bear. VF-11 was attached to CVW-3, which was embarked on the *John F. Kennedy* for several deployments between October 1981 and May 1984, and this photo was probably taken on the last of these. *USN*

Above: Although the F-14A Tomcat had become operational in 1974, it was only over a decade later (1987) that the redoubtable F-4 Phantom II was finally replaced in all US Navy front-line fighter squadrons. Even then, some USMC Reserve squadrons did not give up their Phantoms until 1992. When the USS *Nimitz* sailed to the Mediterranean on her first operational deployment in July 1976, her Air Wing (CVW-8) included the F-4J Phantom IIs of VF-74 'Be-deviliers', one of which is seen straining on the catapult ready for launching. However, this association was short-lived as when the ship deployed again in September 1977, VF-74 had been replaced by VF-41 'Black Aces' flying the new F-14A Tomcat. *NHHC*

Opposite above: The second Nimitz class carrier was the USS *Dwight D. Eisenhower* (CVN-69), which commissioned on 18 October 1977 and sailed on her first operational deployment in January 1979 with CVW-7 embarked. The ship was in the Mediterranean in June 1982 when Israel invaded the Lebanon in response to Palestinian Liberation Organisation (PLO) activities and Syrian forces became involved in an intensely fought war, which was stopped by a ceasefire agreement on 22 June. US Navy carriers were deployed to safeguard American interests and later to support the peacekeeping force (which included US troops) established in August 1982. This photo was taken on 29 June 1982, when the USS *Independence* (CV-62) arrived to relieve the *Dwight D. Eisenhower* (nearest the camera), which, among other actions, had been involved in the evacuation of US Embassy staff from Beirut. *NARA/NMNA*

Opposite below: The crowded flight deck of the USS *Kitty Hawk* (CV-63) in 1980, showing various aircraft of CVW-15. At that time, the Air Wing comprised two squadrons of F-14A Tomcats (VF-51, VF-111), two squadrons of A-7E Corsair IIs (VA-22, VA-94), one squadron of A-6E Intruders (VA-52), and also included some tanker KA-6Es, one AEW detachment with E-2C Hawkeyes (VAW-114), one photo recon detachment with RF-8G Crusaders (VFP-63 Net.1), one EW squadron with EA-6B Growlers (VAQ-135), an EW detachment with EA-3B Skywarriors (VQ-1 Det), an ASW squadron with S-3A Vikings (VS-21), and an ASW helicopter squadron with SH-03H Sea Kings (HS-8). The composition of the squadrons and detachments varied but the total aircraft complement was normally a maximum of ninety-two. *US Defense Imagery*

Above: The jet-powered S-3A Viking had entered service just as the Vietnam War was ending and formed an integral part of the CV carrier air wings, providing far-ranging ASW protection for the ship and its task force. This line-up of Vikings belongs to VS-21 'Fighting Red Tails' aboard the USS *Enterprise* (CVN-65) in 1984, when they formed part of CVW-11. In fact, the squadron had a relatively long association with the ship, embarking for all deployments from May 1984 until March 1990, when the ship decommissioned for a major refit. The Viking proved adaptable for many tasks including in-flight refuelling and the aircraft facing the camera is carrying a pair of underwing pods containing hose and drogue units. Also of note is that the nearest S-3A has a drab grey finish with toned-down markings, a scheme which at that time was replacing the previous standard gloss grey/white colours. *USN*

Opposite above: For close-in ASW work the S-3A Vikings were supported by helicopter detachments flying the SH-3 Sea King. This neat formation is flown by HS-12 'Wyverns' from CVW-5 embarked on the USS *Midway* (CV-41) in 1985. Again, this squadron had a long association with its parent ship, serving aboard *Midway* for no less than sixteen deployments between October 1984 and August 1991. Subsequently, it transferred with the rest of the air wing to the USS *Independence* (CV-62), on which it served until disestablished in 1998, still flying the venerable Sea King. *US Defense Imagery*

Opposite below: On 24 April 1980, US forces launched Operation Eagle Claw – an operation intended to rescue the hostages held at the US Embassy in Tehran since November 1979. The US Navy had two carriers, USS *Nimitz* and USS *Coral Sea*, stationed in the Arabian Sea off the coast of Iran to provide any air cover required. *Nimitz* also embarked the eight RH-53D Sea Stallion helicopters of HM-16 'Sea Hawks' shown here whose function would be to transport the ground troops within Iran once they had been air-landed at a temporary desert airstrip. They were equipped with an in-flight refuelling probe and fitted with sponson-mounted 500-gallon fuel tanks. Capable of carrying up to fifty-five troops, they appeared ideal for the task. Unfortunately, due to a combination of mechanical issues and a fatal accident at the airstrip, the mission was abandoned and only one Sea Stallion made it back to the carrier. *USN*

Above: Operation Eagle Claw was also supported by the USS *Coral Sea* (CV-43). On board was CVW-14, which was tasked with providing air support during the operation when a reaction from the Iranian Air Force could be expected. As Iran flew both F-14 Tomcats and F-4 Phantoms, the US aircraft were given special identification wing markings. These took the form of a red or orange band between two thin black bands. These can be seen on the starboard wings of a VA-196 A-6E Intruder and an F-4J Phantom II of VFMA-323 as they prepare to launch from the *Coral Sea* while off Iran. *USN*

Opposite above: The Iran hostage crisis ended on 20 January 1981 when Ronald Reagan succeeded Jimmy Carter as President of the United States and Iran released the US citizens. The incoming president was a supporter of a strong navy and on taking office implemented a 600-ship plan designed to reverse the cutbacks that followed the Vietnam War and to confront the Soviet Navy, which was also expanding and challenging US naval superiority. Production of the Nimitz class carriers was prioritised and by the end of the decade, another three were in commission. These were the USS *Carl Vinson* (CVN-69, commissioned March 1982), USS *Theodore Roosevelt* (CVN-71, October 1986) and USS *Abraham Lincoln* (CVN-72, November 1989). The latter is shown here conducting sea trials in early 1990 before embarking her air wing (CVW-11) later that year. *USN*

Opposite below: In the 1980s, US carrier aircraft in the Mediterranean were involved in several incidents, some of which resulted in air-to-air combats. On 19 August 1981, a pair of F-14A Tomcats from USS *Nimitz* (CVN-68) was engaged by a pair of Libyan Sukhoi Su-22 fighters, both of which were shot down with Sidewinder missiles. A similar incident occurred on 4 January 1989 when another pair of Tomcats from VF-32 shot down two Libyan MiG-23s. The US aircraft were from CVW-3 aboard the carrier USS *John F. Kennedy* (CV-67), which was nearing the end of a Mediterranean deployment. In this photo, taken at that time, Tomcats of VF-32 'Swordsmen' and VF-14 'Tophatters' are ranged on the after flight deck together with three S-3A Vikings of VS-22 'Checkmates'. *USN*

Above: On 7 October 1985, four Palestine Liberation Front (PLF) militants hijacked the cruise liner *Achille Lauro* off the Egyptian coast and murdered an American citizen, Leon Klinghoffer. Two days later, the hijackers surrendered to the Egyptian authorities, who arranged to fly them to a safe haven in Tunisia aboard an Egyptair Boeing 737. Alerted to this plan, President Reagan ordered the airliner to be intercepted and made to land at a NATO airbase on Sicily. The mission was successfully carried out on the night of 10 October by Tomcats of VF-74 and VF-103, supported by other aircraft of CVW-17 from the USS *Saratoga* (CV-60). Subsequently, most of the hijackers were found guilty in an Italian court and given various prison sentences. This is one of the VF-74 Tomcats aboard *Saratoga* shortly after the interception mission. *USN*

Opposite above: On 5 April 1986, a bomb exploded in a Berlin nightclub, killing three people (including a US serviceman) and injuring over 200 others. In retaliation, the president authorised a significant series of bomb raids against major targets in Libya, which took place in the early hours of 15 April under the code name Operation Eldorado Canyon. Although much publicity was given to the USAF F-111s based in the UK, the US Navy contributed more aircraft from the carriers USS *America* (CV-66) and USS *Coral Sea* (CV-43). This is the scene aboard the USS *America* during that night as she prepares to launch an F-14A Tomcat of VF-102 and an A-7E Corsair II of VA-46 'Clansmen'. Next in line, behind the A-7E, is a USMC EA-6B Growler of VMAQ-2, which was one of several aircraft tasked with jamming communications and radars of the Libyan air defence system. *NMNA*

Opposite below: Operation Eldorado Canyon also saw the combat debut of the new McDonnell F/A-18A Hornet. Aboard the USS *Coral Sea* (CV-43), CVW-13 deployed no less than four Hornet squadrons, two Navy fighter squadrons (VFA-131, VFA-132) and two USMC attack squadrons (VMFA-314, VFMA-323), which are represented by the two examples parked on the edge of *Coral Sea*'s flight deck in January 1986. On the left is an F/A-18 of VFA-131 'Wildcats' and beside it is another from Marine strike fighter squadron VMFA-323 'Death Rattlers'. On the night of 15 April, six Hornets from VFA-131 and VFA-132 fired a total of twenty-four Shrike and HARM anti-radar missiles, severely incapacitating the ground air defences. *USN*

Chapter 8

Hot Action after the Cold War
1990-2003

Despite the nominal end of the Cold War in 1990 with the coming of Glasnost and the break-up of the Soviet Union, the world was not a safer place. In 1990, Iraqi forces invaded Kuwait and in response, an allied coalition was formed to carry out Operation Desert Shield in preparation for Desert Storm. The latter was the code name allocated to liberate Kuwait and drive out the occupying Iraqi forces. US naval aircraft from up to six carriers in the region played a vital role in this war, which concluded successfully at the end of February 1991. Thereafter, a no-fly zone was established over southern Iraq, and US Navy aircraft participated in its enforcement for the next decade under Operation Southern Watch.

In the mid-1990s, the break-up of the Soviet Union was followed by the break-up of the former Yugoslavia, which involved civil war strife between its various ethnic groups. Eventually, this precipitated action by NATO and UN peacekeeping forces and, at times, the establishment of no-fly zones (operation Deny Flight) and air support for ground forces (Operation Endeavour). NATO aircraft based on Italian airfields supplied much of the air support needed for these actions. However, US 6th Fleet carriers often assisted and their EW aircraft, such as the EA-6 Prowler, were particularly useful.

The horrific 9/11 attack on New York in September 2001 triggered yet more action by US forces. Operation Enduring Freedom was mounted, in which US and coalition troops entered Afghanistan and, again, carriers were deployed in support. The object was to defeat the Taliban and remove their ability to set up terrorist training camps, and the campaign was to rumble on for almost two decades before the US and their coalition partners withdrew, leaving the Taliban still in place.

In the meantime, the focus moved back to the Middle East, where the perception that Saddam Hussein was in possession of weapons of mass destruction was the reason for the launch of a full-scale invasion of Iraq under the code name Iraqi Freedom, which began on 19 March 2003. US Navy support included five carriers and their task groups deployed in the Red Sea, Persian Gulf and the Arabian Sea. Although Operation Iraqi Freedom was a success in military terms with the toppling of Saddam Hussein and the defeat of Iraqi forces, the aftermath was poorly managed and internal strife and conflict continued until at least 2018. However, the conclusion of the initial invasion in 2003 seems an appropriate point to end this historic review of US naval aviation, although since then there have been exciting developments that may well form the basis of a future account.

When Iraqi forces invaded Kuwait in August 1990, Tomcat-equipped VF-32 joined the USS *John F. Kennedy* (CV-67), which then crossed the North Atlantic and proceeded through the Mediterranean and Suez Canal to the Red Sea. From there, the Tomcats provided CAP over Saudi air bases during Desert Shield but moved back to the Mediterranean in time to take part in Desert Storm, for which VF-32 maintained CAP protection over Western Iraq for the first wave of strikes. In this three-ship formation the aircraft are in standard drab grey finish, but the lead aircraft (coded 101, the squadron commander's aircraft) displays more colourful markings. *US Defense Imagery.*

Above: Also part of CVW-3 aboard the *Kennedy* during the Gulf War were the EA-6B Prowlers of VAQ-130 'Zappers'. These aircraft, along with other US Navy and USAF EW assets, played a vital role in suppressing Iraqi air defence systems during Desert Storm. In this image one of a pair of Prowlers is being refuelled by a USAF KC-135R Stratotanker while, in the background, another Prowler is taking on fuel from a KA-6E, which is using a buddy refuelling pack. *USN*

Opposite above: Although led by US forces, Desert Storm involved a coalition of forces from other nations, as is illustrated in this view of the USS *Ranger* (CV-61) refuelling the Netherlands frigate *Jacob van Heemskerck* in early January 1991, just before the commencement of the Desert Storm air strikes. On *Ranger*'s deck are the aircraft of CVW-2, made up of two squadrons of F-14A Tomcats and two squadrons of A-6E Intruders as well as other support units. When Desert Storm commenced on 16 January 1991, the Navy launched 228 sorties from *Ranger* and USS *Midway* (CV 41) in the Persian Gulf, from USS *Theodore Roosevelt* (CVN 71) en route to the Gulf, and from USS *John F. Kennedy* (CV 67), USS *Saratoga* (CV 60), and USS *America* (CV 66) in the Red Sea and Mediterranean. *USN*

Opposite below: By 1990, when Desert Shield operations began, the F/A-18 was well established aboard US carriers. These two Hornets are F/A-18C variants, which featured improved avionics and were able to carry AIM-120 AMRAAM and AGM-65 Maverick-guided munitions. They are flown by VFA-81 'Sunliners' deployed as part of CVW-17 aboard the USS *Saratoga* (CV-60), which was the centrepiece of a Red Sea battle group from August 1990 to March 1991. Hornets of VFA-81 scored the US Navy's first (and only) air-to-air combat victories when they shot down two Iraqi MiG-21s on the first day of Desert Storm. *USN*

Above: Operation Desert Storm in 1991 was the swansong of the venerable carrier USS *Midway* (CV-41), which had first commissioned in 1945. Too small to operate the F-14A Tomcat, her air wing (CVW-5) included three squadrons of F/A-18A Hornets and two of A-6E/KA-6D Intruders. Despite her age and limitations, she was in the forefront of the action as flagship of Force Zulu, which at times also included the carriers USS *Ranger* (CV-61), *America* (CV-66) and *Theodore Roosevelt* (CVN-71). This overhead view was taken at Pearl Harbor in November 1991 as the *Midway* was on her final voyage home before being decommissioned in 1992. On the other side of the pier is the larger Forrestal class carrier USS *Independence* (CV-62), which was proceeding westbound as *Midway*'s replacement as the forward-based carrier at Yokosuka, Japan. *USN*

Opposite above: During the mid-1990s, in addition to continuing issues in the Middle East, open warfare broke out in the Balkans following the break-up of the previous Yugoslav republic, and this included horrific incidents of genocide. Consequently, a number of UN peacekeeping forces were established in the area and, to assist their mission and reduce civilian casualties, a no-fly zone over Bosnia and Herzegovina was established (Operation Deny Flight) and was in force from April 1993 until December 1995. Although NATO squadrons based in Italy were mostly responsible for enforcing the no-fly zone, they were at times assisted by the USS *Theodore Roosevelt* with CVW-8 embarked. This F-14A Tomcat of VF-84 is about to be launched for a Deny Flight patrol at the end of April 1993. *NARA*

Opposite below: During the 1990s, the US Navy commissioned four more Nimitz class nuclear-powered aircraft carriers. The first of these was the USS *George Washington* (CVN-73), which was commissioned on 4 July 1992. As shown here, the Navy organised these commissioning ceremonies on a grand scale and apart from the ship's officers and crew, many others here lining the flight deck included family members, shipyard workers, civic dignitaries and Navy top brass. The carrier's starboard elevators have been lowered to provide access and seating in addition to the rows of chairs on the quayside. *USN*

Above: With an air wing comprising eighty or more aircraft and also operating in conjunction with other carriers or land-based air assets, the monitoring and control of flying activities was a complex affair. A large carrier, such as the *George Washington*, would have its own air traffic control centre with a team of controllers responsible for co-ordinating and controlling air movements over a large area. One of the Navy controllers is here monitoring one of several radar displays while to his right is a screen showing the position of aircraft in the carrier's landing pattern. This photo was taken c.1996 and shows a typical analogue radar display of the period, which appears crude when compared to the high definition digital displays with overlaid data in use today. *USN*

Opposite above: Between January and July 1996, the USS *George Washington* was deployed to the US 6th Fleet in the Mediterranean and among its tasks was the support of Operation Endeavour. This involved NATO troops acting in a UN-mandated peacekeeping role in Bosnia and Herzegovina under the title IFOR (Implementation Force). Embarked on the carrier was CVW-7, which included the EA-6B Prowlers of Tactical Electronic Warfare Squadron 140 (VAQ-140 'Patriots'), one of which is here on patrol over Bosnia. Noticeable are the AN/ALQ-99 jamming pods, of which EA-6B normally carried three, one under each wing and one under the fuselage centreline. The streamlined pod on top of the tail fin contains receivers for monitoring equipment. *USN*

Opposite below: The USS *Carl Vinson* (CVN-70) had commissioned in 1982 and was named after a prominent Democrat politician who had given much support to the Navy. Although he died in 1981, he would have been heartened to see this demonstration of naval air power flown by the ship's air wing (CVW-14) over the Persian Gulf in 1994. Visible are F-14D Tomcats from VF-1 'Red Rippers' and VF-31 'Tomcatters'; an S-3B Viking from VS-35 'Blue Wolves'; an F/A-18C(N) Hornet from VFA-25 'Fist of the Fleet' and VFA-113 'Stingers'; an EA-6B Prowler from VAQ-139 'Cougars'; an E-2C Hawkeye from VAW-113 'Black Eagles' and an A-6E Intruder from VA-196 'Main Battery'. All in all, a striking illustration of the air power deployed by a single air wing. *NARA*

A pair of F/A-18C Hornets flown by VFA-37 'Bulls' deployed aboard the USS *Enterprise* (CVN-65) between November 1998 and May 1999. This version of the Hornet had been in service since 1989, but these examples are F/A-18C(N) variants upgraded for the night attack role. Modifications included the addition of an AN/AAS-38A Nite Hawk FLIR system providing a Laser Target Designation facility for precision-guided munitions (PGM) such as the GBU-12 Paveway II 500lb bomb visible under the wings of these Hornets. *USN*

Opposite: The events of 11 September 2001 (9/11) triggered retaliatory action against the Taliban forces in Afghanistan, which officially began on 7 October 2001 under the code name Enduring Freedom. The invasion of Afghanistan was again carried out by a US-led coalition and initial air support came from carriers deployed in the Arabian Sea including the USS *Theodore Roosevelt* (CVN-71). This close-up view shows the ship's island superstructure and parked on deck are aircraft of CVW-1, including F-14B Tomcats of VF-102 'Diamondbacks' and two E-2C Hawkeyes of VAW-123 'Screwtops'. At this stage, the Tomcat was nearing the end of its career and the other three fighter and attack squadrons on board were equipped with the F/A-18C Hornets. *USN*

Above: The scene aboard the *Theodore Roosevelt* as one of the VAW-123 E-3C Hawkeyes is about to be launched. The E-2C variant can be easily identified by the prominent dorsal scoop just behind the cockpit. This was needed to provide cooling air for the substantial increase in the power and variety of the improved radar, communications and computing equipment installed in this variant. Even after the E-2C was introduced in 1973, the original APS-120 radar was successively replaced by upgraded versions and at the time of this photo, 2001, it was the APS-145 ARPS (Advanced Radar Processing System) with a range of over 250 miles and inbuilt ECCM to defeat jamming attempts. With a wingspan of just over 80 feet, the Hawkeye (and its C-2 Greyhound transport derivative) is the largest aircraft to operate from the Navy's carriers. *NARA*

Opposite above: The Grumman C-2A Greyhound was developed in the 1960s for the COD transport role and was based in the E-2A Hawkeye. It used the same wings, engines and tail unit mated to a new higher-volume fuselage that could accommodate up to thirty-nine passengers and up to 15,000lb of cargo (maximum 10,000lb for carrier operations). Entering service with Fleet Tactical Support Squadron 50 (VRC-50) in 1966, it was still operating in 2003 at the time of the Iraq War. This C-2A is landing aboard the USS *Theodore Roosevelt* (CVN-71) during Operation Iraqi Freedom and belongs to Detachment 5 of VRC-40 'Rawhides'. It was one of two C-2As deployed aboard the ship from January to May 2003. *USN*

Opposite below: By 2001, the Sikorsky SH-60F Seahawk had long since replaced the SH-3 Sea King aboard the US Navy's carriers. Its prime role function was as an ASW platform but it was also useful for search and rescue (SAR) missions and for transferring stores and equipment during vertical replenishment manoeuvres. Each carrier air wing usually included six SH-60F Seahawks as well as two HH-60H Rescue Hawks, the latter stripped of ASW gear and fitted for SAR and with machine guns and defensive aids for insertion of special forces. This SH-60F is from HS-8 'Eightballers', assigned to the USS *John C. Stennis* (CVN-74) during Operation Enduring Freedom, April 2002. The *John C. Stennis* was the seventh Nimitz class in service and commissioned on 9 December 1995. *USN*

Above: Commissioned on 25 July 1998, the USS *Harry S. Truman* (CVN-75) was the next Nimitz class carrier to enter service. Pictured in December 2002 while deployed in the Mediterranean with the US Sixth Fleet, the ship had previously contributed to Operations Enduring Freedom and Southern Watch. On deck are ranged the aircraft of CVW-3, including the F-14B Tomcats of VF-32 and F/A-18A/C Hornets of Navy squadrons VFA-37 and VFA-105 'Gunslingers', and USMC squadron VMFA-115 'Silver Eagles'. Others visible include E-2C Hawkeyes (VAW-126), S-3B Vikings (VS-22) and SH-60F Seahawks (HS-7). Following *Truman*'s commissioning, the USS *Independence* (CV-62) was retired meaning that, by then, all four of the original Forrestal class had been decommissioned. *USN*

Opposite above: Originally designed and produced by McDonnell Douglas, the F/A-18 Hornet and its derivatives became a Boeing product after the merger of the two companies in 1997. The Boeing F/A-18E (and the two-seat F/A-18F) Super Hornet appeared to be a scaled-up standard Hornet but in fact was virtually a new and more capable aircraft. Flown as a prototype in 1995, the Super Hornet began to reach front-line squadrons from 2001 onwards. One of these was VF-41, which replaced its long-serving F-14 Tomcats with F/A-18 Super Hornets in 2002 and subsequently deployed with CVW-11 aboard the USS *Nimitz* (CVN-68) during Operation Iraqi Freedom. Two of its aircraft are shown preparing to launch with the Australian frigate HMAS *Adelaide* alongside acting as plane guard in April 2003. *USN*

Opposite below: In the second half of 2002, the USS *Abraham Lincoln* deployed to the Arabian Sea and Persian Gulf, initially in support of Operations Enduring Freedom and then Iraqi Freedom. The embarked air wing was CVW-14, which included VFA-115 'Eagles' equipped with the new F/A-18E Super Hornet. In fact, this squadron was the first to receive the Super Hornet and the first to fly it on combat operations. To aid identity, squadron commanders' aircraft were given a more colourful treatment than the standard overall grey and, in this case, the all-black tail fins bear the carrier's modex (NF) in yellow lettering and the squadron insignia in yellow and white. The national markings are in full colour (red, white and blue). *USN*

The FA-18E/F was intended as a replacement for the F-14 Tomcat and by 2003, that programme was well under way (the last operational Tomcats were retired in 2006). This F-14D landing aboard the USS *Constellation* (CV-64) in May 2003 belongs to VF-2 'Bounty Hunters'. During the Iraqi War the squadron flew a wide range of missions including reconnaissance, close-air support, CAP, and strike missions. Note the pod under the nose, which contains the Tactical Camera System (TCS) and the sensor for the ALQ-100 Infra Red Search and Track (IRST) system. VF-2 re-equipped with F/A-18E/F Super Hornets at the end of 2003. *USN*

The initial military objectives of Operation Iraqi Freedom had been achieved by the end of April 2003 and at that point the carrier USS *Abraham Lincoln* (CVN-72) was already proceeding home following her involvement in the actions. On 1 May, President George W. Bush flew out to the carrier aboard an S-3B Viking of VS-35 'Blue Wolves', which used the privileged call sign 'NAVY ONE'. This was the first time a serving US president had made an arrested carrier landing although others had boarded by helicopter, and his father, George H.W. Bush, was a naval pilot in the Second World War. Once aboard the carrier, the president addressed the ship's crew and made his famous 'Mission Accomplished' speech. Events were soon to show that it was an optimistic concept, but for now, it seems an appropriate point to close this review of US naval aviation since 1945. *NMNA*

Chapter 9

Supporting the Front Line

Until the formation of the United States Air Force in 1947, the US Navy and US Army had maintained their own independent air transport services. In 1948, the two organisations were combined to form the Military Air Transport Service although the Navy squadrons retained their original identities. This arrangement continued until 1966 when the Navy withdrew, partly due to a lack of available pilots brought about by the demands of the Vietnam War. Shore-based naval transport aircraft reverted to naval control for what were termed Operational Support Airlift (OSA) missions. In the decades following the Second World War, Navy transport aircraft were invariably military versions of standard civilian airliners (mostly the various Douglas DC models), the main exemption being the supremely adaptable C-130 Hercules, which was also used in numbers by the USMC. In the jet age, the Navy acquired variants of the popular Douglas DC-9 as the C-9B, and the Boeing 737 as the C-40.

The pilot shortage referred to above illustrates one of the major factors in maintaining a strong front-line force aboard the carriers – the need for a steady supply of well-trained pilots and other aircrew. Since 1972 that has been the responsibility of a unified Naval Air Training Command, which brought together a previous organisation involving various specialist commands. In 1944, at the peak of wartime operations, the US Navy trained a staggering 21,067 pilots but, by 1948, this had fallen to a mere 446. However, from 1950 onwards, the numbers rose to a yearly average of around 1,400 pilots, although that figured doubled in the latter half of the 1950s and again in the Vietnam War period.

The training syllabus followed a universal pattern of primary and advanced training followed by a period of operational conversion, usually with one of the Readiness Carrier Air Wings (RCVW) or a Fleet Replacement Squadron. Initial training in live carrier operations was carried out aboard one of the older carriers set aside for the task. Notable amongst these was the USS *Lexington* (CVT-16), which undertook this role for twenty-two years between 1969 and 1991 before she was retired and replaced by the USS *Forrestal*.

Since 1954, primary training has been carried out using the piston-engined Beech T-34B Mentor and it successor, the turboprop-powered T-34C Turbo Mentor. It was only at the start of the twenty-first century that a replacement in the form of the T-6B Texan II was introduced, although being a new design it featured the advanced digital cockpit of the type that newly qualified pilots would find in modern front-line aircraft. A basic jet trainer in the form of the Rockwell T-2 Buckeye entered service in 1959 and again had a long forty-five-year career. Advanced training was usually carried out in two-seat versions of combat aircraft such as the Grumman Cougar and Douglas Skyhawk but, since 1992, this has been the province of the T-45 Goshawk, a purpose-designed jet trainer based on the British BAe Hawk.

One of the most useful tools in helping to recruit new pilots is the US Navy Flight Demonstration Team, better known as the Blue Angels. First formed in 1946 with Grumman Hellcats, they have since flown virtually every naval front-line fighter, including the current F/A-18E/F Super Hornet.

The Douglas DC-3 and its military counterparts is probably one of the most famous aircraft ever built. In USAAF service it became the C-47, while US Navy aircraft were designated R4D, serving from 1941 until well into the 1970s. In 1949, Douglas flew a prototype of the much-improved Super DC-3 (DC-3S), which featured a stretched fuselage, more powerful engines, a taller tail fin to improve engine-out handling, and a reduced wingspan with squared-off tips. Despite an enhanced performance, it failed to achieve commercial success. However, in 1951, the US Navy was impressed enough to order ninety-eight of its standard R4Ds to be converted to the new configuration as the R4D-8 (C-117D after 1962) and the last of these was only retired in 1976. This is the prototype Super DC-3 undergoing Navy trials in 1951. *NARA*

Above: In the post-war decades the US Navy continued to operate transports derived from the highly successful range of Douglas airliners. The four-engined Douglas DC-4 had flown in 1942 and subsequently entered service with the USAAF as the C-54 Skymaster, while naval variants (of which over 200 eventually entered service) were designated R5D, some of which remained in service until the early 1970s. The prototype of the larger DC-6 flew in 1946 and military versions, named Liftmaster, were the USAF C-118 and the US Navy's R6D, with sixty-one of the latter being ordered. One of the first squadrons to receive the R6D-1 was VR-1 'Star Lifters' and one of their aircraft is shown here in 1960. *NHHC*

Opposite above: In the 1950s, VR-1 also received a number of Convair R4Y transports, which were a military version of the successful Convair CV-340 airliner (USAF version was the C-131 Samaritan). The US Navy obtained a total of thirty-six R4Y-1s as well as a single R4Y-1Z VIP twenty-four-seat VIP transport and two R4Y-2s based on the more refined CV-440 (several R4Y-1s were later upgraded to R4Y-2 standard). All were redesignated as C-131s in 1962. The USAF also ordered over 300 crew and navigation trainers based on the CV-240/340 as the Convair T-29. Ten were loaned to the US Navy in 1963 and used by VT-29 until the early 1970s at NAS Corpus Christi but retained their T-29B Air Force designations. Photo shows a smart looking C-131F of VR-1 in 1965, when the squadron was based at the Naval Air Facility, Washington DC. *NMNA*

Opposite below: From November 1952, the US Navy acquired fifty-one Lockheed L1049 Super Constellations as R7V-1 (later C-121J) transports although many were subsequently transferred to the USAF. The Super Constellation was also adapted as the WV-2 Warning Star (see Chapter 6) and 142 of these were ordered, entering service from 1953 onwards. Finally, in September 1954, the Navy took delivery of the first of two R7V-2s powered by four 5,550eshp Pratt & Whitney YT34 turboprops housed in extended nacelles. This resulted a substantial boost to performance and cruising speed increased from 259mph of the standard R7V-1 to 430mph. However, the YT34 turboprop proved troublesome and after a short trial period the two aircraft were returned to Lockheed, who used one as a test bed for Allison 501D turboprops, which eventually powered the Electra airliner and its offspring, the P-3 Orion (see Chapter 6). *NMNA*

Above: In 1942, the US Navy began studies to develop a large, long-range, pressurised transport, which also interested Pan American Airways. In the event, only two examples of what was to become the Lockheed R6O Constitution were built and these flew in November 1946 and June 1948. Both were delivered to transport squadron VR-44, who flew them until 1953, while Pan Am never placed any orders. The two Constitutions were the largest aircraft ever flown by the US Navy and the upper half of the double bubble fuselage cross section could accommodate up to ninety-two passengers while the lower deck was used for cargo (although could be configured to carry another seventy-six passengers). The Constitution was underpowered for its size, and consequently, the use of rocket-assisted take-offs was investigated, as seen here. *NARA*

Opposite above: Military versions of the very successful McDonnell Douglas DC-9 jet airliner were ordered as the C-9A Nightingale for the USAF and the C-9B Skytrain II for the Navy. The first C-9B was delivered in 1973 and the last of the seventeen aircraft ordered was delivered on 28 October 1982 (this was actually the last DC-9 to be built). In addition, at least six ex-airline DC-9s were obtained. The C-9B shown here is one of four flown by West Coast-based VR-57 'Conquistadors', which began operating the C-9B in 1978 and, among other tasks, was based in Germany in 1990/91 to support Operations Desert Shield and Desert Storm. In 2005, the squadron would re-equip with the Boeing C-40, the military version of the Boeing 737. *USN*

Opposite below: The private venture Beechcraft Model 45 Mentor was first flown in December 1948 and it later entered service with the USAF as the T-34A Mentor in 1954. The Navy version was the the T-34B, ordered in June 1954, and a total of 423 had been delivered by October 1957. The Mentor became the Navy's primary trainer for the next twenty years before it was succeeded by the T-34C Turbo Mentor, in which the 225hp Continental O-470-13 piston engine was replaced by a Pratt & Whitney PT6A-25 turboprop de-rated to 400shp. Entering service in 1977, the Turbo Mentor was retired from 2002 onwards as the new Beechcraft T-6B Texan II entered service under the Joint Primary Aircraft Training System (JPATS) whereby both Air Force and Navy trainee pilots undergo a common syllabus until streamed for advanced training. The aircraft shown here is an early production T-34B allocated to the Instructor Basic Training Unit (IBTU) in 1955. *NARA*

A batch of single-seat Lockheed F-80C Shooting Stars were obtained in 1948 for use as advanced jet trainers (designated TO-1/TV-1). Subsequently, no fewer than 699 two-seat T-33s were procured for use by the US Navy and USMC under the designation TV-2. However, the Navy still needed a jet trainer that could be flown from aircraft carriers. Consequently, Lockheed produced a modified version that became the TV-2 (T-1A after 1962) SeaStar, which entered service in 1956. The airframe and undercarriage were strengthened to cope with catapult launches and arrested landings. A raised cockpit profile gave a better view for the rear seat occupant, while take-off and landing speeds were reduced by the use of leading edge flaps and a boundary layer control system. The SeaStar entered service in 1957, although by 1960, it was no longer used for carrier training. The company owned prototype SeaStar is seen alongside the earlier TV-1 (T-33) on which it was based. *NARA*.

The North American (Rockwell) T-2 Buckeye was the Navy's first purpose-designed jet trainer. First flown in 1958, the T-2A was powered by a single 3,400lb.s.t. J34 turbojet and entered service with Basic Training Group Seven (BTG-7) in July 1959. In 1962, Rockwell flew the twin-engined T-2B, in which a pair of 3,000lb.s.t. J60 turbojets replaced the J34, substantially boosting performance. Subsequently, the T-2C entered service in 1969 powered by a pair of GE J85 turbojets of a similar power rating but better fuel efficiency. The T-2C eventually replaced all the earlier variants and only began to be retired in 2004. In this 1980 view the T-2C in the foreground flies formation on a North American T-39 Sabreliner, which was used to train pilots and flight officers in the use of various radar systems. Both aircraft belonged to Pensacola-based VT-10 'Cosmic Cats' (later changed to 'Wildcats'). NMNA

Above: In the 1950s and early 60s, advanced training was carried out on a two-seat trainer version of the swept-wing Cougar (F9F-8T/TF-9J). Its replacement was a two-seat version of the A-4 Skyhawk, initially the TA-4F and later TA-4J. A total of 555 two-seat Skyhawks were built and many of the earlier TA-4Fs were converted to TA-4Js. In 1966, the first unit to receive the TA-4F was VA-125 'Rough Raiders', based at NAS Lemoore. It is estimated that at least 11,000 naval aviators trained and qualified on the TA-4 before it began to be replaced in the training role by the T-45 Goshawk from 1992 onwards, although many were later flown by 'aggressor' units for dissimilar combat training. This TA-4J from VT-7 'Eagles' is visiting the USS *Carl Vinson* in April 1984. *NMNA*

Opposite above: The T-45 Goshawk was based on the British Aerospace Hawk advanced trainer, first flown in 1971. US Navy interest dated back to 1978 but it was not until 1988 that a prototype T-45 Goshawk finally took to the air and this featured many modifications to the basic Hawk to suit it for carrier operations. The T-45 was produced by Boeing (McDonnell Douglas) in St Louis using several BAe-supplied major components and entered US Navy service with VT-21 'Redhawks' in 1992. The original T-45A featured a traditional analogue cockpit but the T-45C introduced in 1997 featured a digital 'glass' cockpit and subsequently all the earlier Goshawks were brought up to that standard. This T-45C making a touch-and-go aboard the USS *John C. Stennis* (CVN-74) in March 2003 belongs to VT-7, part of Training Wing One (TW-1). *USN*

Opposite below: The famous Blue Angels aerobatic team (now officially known as the US Navy Flight Demonstration Team) was formed in April 1946 flying Grumman F9F-5 Hellcats, but almost immediately transitioned to the sleeker F8F-1 Bearcat. At the time, the objective was to generate interest and support for naval aviation amongst the public and politicians. However, it later proved be an excellent recruiting platform and many US naval pilots were first inspired by seeing the team in action. The Angels' first jets were F9F-2 Panthers, which they flew from 1949 to the end of 1954, when they were replaced by the swept-wing F9F-8 Cougars shown here. *NARA*

In 1957, the Blue Angels were re-equipped with the Grumman F11F-1 Tiger, which, although had a relatively short career with front-line squadrons, was flown by the team for eleven years (1957–68). Its replacement was the mighty F-4J Phantom II, which lasted until 1974 when the team changed to A-4F Skyhawk. The delta-winged Skyhawk was highly manoeuvrable and more economic to fly and maintain. It was then twelve years before another change took place in 1986, this time to the Navy's latest front-line fighter, the F/A-18 Hornet (and still flying the advanced F/A-18E/F Super Hornet today). The Blue Angels' speciality has always been flying complex manoeuvres while maintaining very tight formations, as illustrated by this spectacular fly-by with two aircraft inverted. *ASM*

Chapter 10

Pushing the Boundaries

By the end of the war in 1945, the US Navy and the US Army Air Force (later USAF) saw that advances in the science and technologies of aeronautics could provide substantial benefits in the design and production of military aircraft. Consequently, they were willing to team up with the civilian National Advisory Council for Aeronautics (NACA – a forerunner of the present NASA) to fund research into high-speed flight. The newly formed US Air Force perhaps stole the limelight when their rocket-powered air-launched Bell X-1 became the first aircraft to fly faster than the speed of sound, on 14 October 1947. However, in the meantime, the US Navy had already hit the headlines, on 20 August 1947, when their jet-powered Douglas Skystreak took the world air speed record (which could not be claimed by the X-1 as it could not take off and land under its own power), and the swept-wing, rocket-powered Skyrocket became the first aircraft to exceed Mach 2.0. Many of the pilots involved in these and other research projects subsequently became astronauts with NASA. In fact, Neil Armstrong, the first man on the moon, was a naval pilot who had flown Panther jets in Korea. Although not a direct product of these research programmes, the delta-winged Douglas F4D Skyray prototype interceptor showed considerable speed potential and allowed the Navy to reclaim the world air speed record once again, in October 1953.

The new high-performance jet aircraft of the 1940s and 50s were larger and heavier than their piston-engined predecessors, and could not operate from the smaller escort carriers that had previously provided air cover for convoys and amphibious operations. Consequently, in 1950, the US Navy raised a specification for a vertical take-off research aircraft with the potential to be developed as an operational fighter. Two companies, Lockheed and Convair, produced prototypes, but the project was cancelled in 1955 and it was not until 1971 that a successful V/STOL combat aircraft entered US service in the form of the British-designed AV-8A Harrier. Although the AV-8A and its successor, the AV-8B Harrier II, were ordered in large numbers by the US Marine Corps, none were acquired by the US Navy.

Convair was also involved in another project that resulted in a jet-powered seaplane fighter. This flew as the delta-winged XF2Y-1 Sea Dart in 1953. Again, the object was to provide air cover for amphibious landings and deploy from mobile bases that would not then require the presence of an aircraft carrier. Instead of conventional floats, the Sea Dart employed retractable hydro skis, which, after testing various configurations, actually worked quite well in practice. Had Sea Dart squadrons ever been deployed they would have needed the logistic support provided by large flying boat transports such as the turboprop-powered R3Y Tradewind (another Convair product), which was produced in small numbers for service between 1956 and 1958.

The ultimate US Navy flying boat was the jet-powered Martin P6M-1 SeaMaster. Flown in 1955, it was intended as a nuclear strike bomber operating from mobile bases and would rival the Air Force's B-52. However, like many of the ambitious projects launched in the 1950s, a combination of technical issues and financial constraints resulted in the cancellation of the project in 1959.

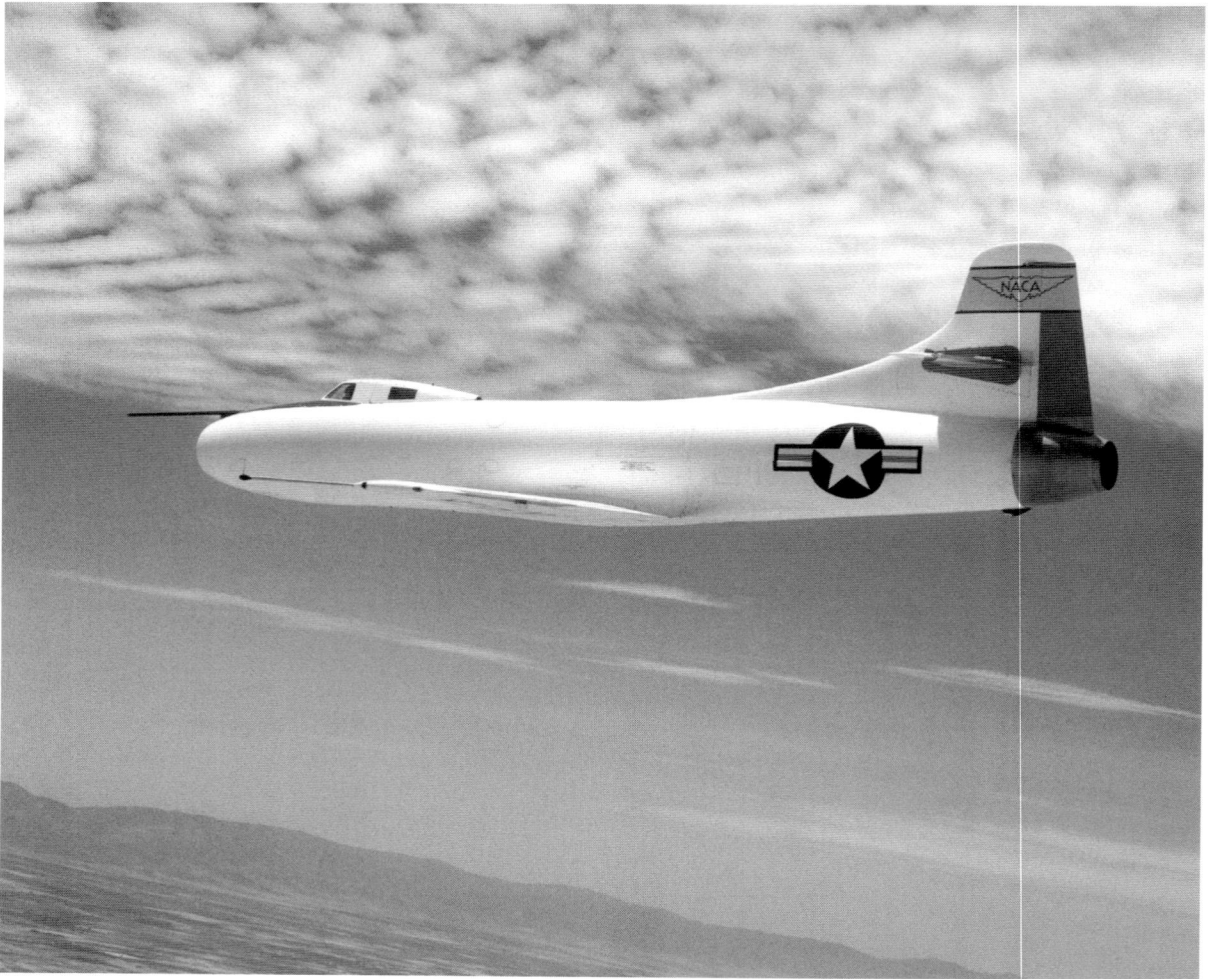

Opposite: The Douglas D-558-1 Skystreak was the result of the collaboration started in 1944 between the US Navy and NACA. The turbojet-powered Skystreak's first flight occurred on 15 April 1947 and, after some initial problems, demonstrated speeds in excess of Mach 0.85. Encouraged by this, the Navy decided to use the aircraft for a successful attempt on the world air speed record on 20 August 1947, achieving a speed of 640.663mph, which was comfortably in excess of the previous record of 623.738mph set by a modified Lockheed P-80 Shooting Star. Only five days later, the second prototype was piloted to a new record of 650.796mph and, apart from being great technical achievements, the record-breaking flights were a tremendous boost to the Navy's prestige. *NASA*

The Skystreak was followed by the swept-wing D-558-2 Skyrocket, intended for research into supersonic flight. Its design featured a single 3,000lb.s.t. J34 turbojet for normal flight operations, with provision for a 6,000lb thrust rocket motor for high-speed flight. The prototype first flew (on jet power only) on 4 February 1948 and the third prototype, completed with the rocket engine installed, exceeded Mach 1 on 24 June 1949. Subsequently, both the first two prototypes were converted for air-launched operations with the turbojet removed to make room for more rocket fuel. The mother aircraft was the Navy version of the B-29 Superfortress, designated as the P2B-1S. Using this combination, the Skyrocket logged some spectacular achievements, reaching a maximum altitude of 85,235 feet, and on another occasion was the first aircraft to exceed Mach 2 (in a dive from 72,000 feet). *NARA*

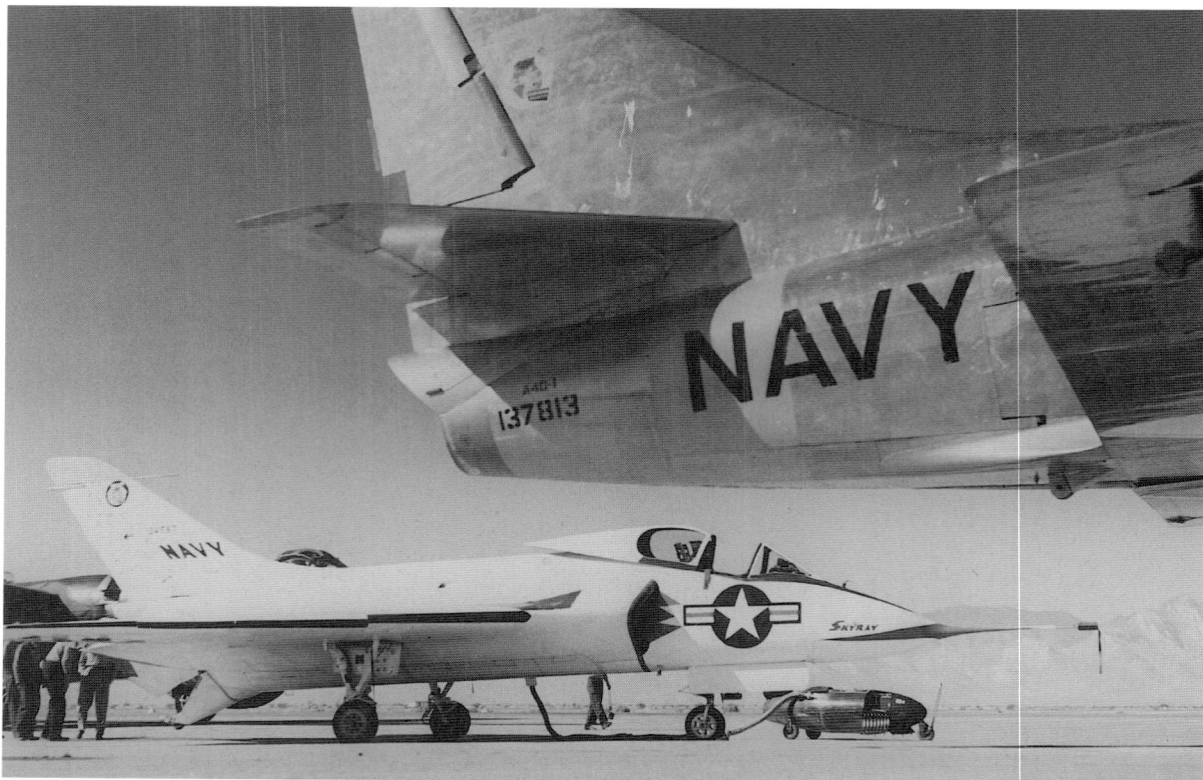

By September 1953, the official FIA world air speed record had been raised successively to 735.7mph, which was held by the British Supermarine Swift. In the meantime, high-speed testing of the US Navy's new delta-winged interceptor, the Douglas XF4D-1 Skyray, powered by an afterburning Westinghouse XJ40-WE-8, showed considerable promise and on 3 October 1953, a record attempt was made. Using the second prototype (BuNo 124587, shown here), a speed of 752.944mph was officially recorded and this was the first time the record had been held by a carrier-capable aircraft. Although the record was overtaken only three weeks later by a USAF F-100C Super Sabre, which recorded 755.1mph, it was nevertheless a notable demonstration of the capabilities of the latest US Navy aircraft. *NARA*

Opposite: The new breed of jet fighters coming into service in the late 1940s could not be operated from the wartime escort carriers, but the increasing power available from the developing jet and turbo prop engines raised the possibility of a vertical take-off fighter. Convair was one of two companies to respond to a US Navy 1950 specification for a vertical take-off and landing (VTOL) research aircraft capable of being developed into an operational escort fighter. The result was the tail-sitting Convair XFY-1, powered by a 5,850ehp Allison YT-40-6 turboprop driving a Curtiss-Wright 16ft diameter contra-rotating prop. Short-span delta wings were attached to the truncated fuselage, which also featured large dorsal and ventral fins, and the tips of the wings and fins provided attachment points for the four castoring wheels. *NARA*

Following indoor tethered trials, the XFY-1 eventually made a full transition to horizontal flight on 2 November 1954, and then landed tail first inside a 50ft square. This was a very significant achievement, but subsequent tests confirmed that consistently landing safely onto a small landing area was fraught with difficulties. Also by then it was realised that the turboprop-powered aircraft's performance was not good enough to enable successful interceptions of bombers approaching at 600mph. Consequently, the programme was cancelled after some forty hours of test flying. *NARA*

Opposite: Lockheed's response to the vertical take-off fighter project was the XFV-1, which was also a tail-sitter powered by the 5,850ehp Allison YT-40-6. A pair of short-span straight wings were attached to the fuselage and a cruciform tail assembly provided mounting points on the wheels. However, it was felt that the XT-40-A-6 engine was not powerful enough to allow safe vertical take-offs and landings (a more powerful XT-40-14 was planned when available) and so the prototype was fitted with a temporary fixed undercarriage to allow test flying in a conventional mode. The official first flight took place on 16 June 1954 (it had previously briefly lifted off during fast taxi trials). Although transitions were made from conventional to vertical flight modes and back again, no vertical take-offs or landings had been attempted when the project was cancelled in June 1955. *NARA*

In response to a requirement for a seaplane fighter to provide air support for amphibious operations, Convair developed the XF2Y-1 (later named Sea Dart), which was based on the company's delta-winged F-102 developed for the Air Force. The main differences were that the Sea Dart was twin-engined (initially two 3,400lb.s.t. J34 turbojets mounted above the rear fuselage) and to enable water operations it was fitted with a pair of retractable hydro skis. The official first flight was made in April 1953, but due to the lack of an area-ruled fuselage and underperformance of the engines, the XF2Y-1 did not achieve the specified supersonic performance (although the later YF2Y-1 did exceed Mach 1 in a dive, but was then lost in an accident in November 1954). By then the original Navy requirement had evaporated, but the remaining XF2Y-1 and second YF2Y-1 were involved in trials with various hydro-ski configurations until 1957. This is the original XF2Y-1 undergoing trials off San Diego. *NARA*

The Convair Tradewind was originally conceived as a long-range patrol flying boat capable of ASW operations. Powered by four 5,850ehp Allison YT-40-4 turboprops, the prototype flew on 18 April 1950, but was lost in an accident in July 1953. In the meantime, orders had been placed for a transport version (R3Y-1) and a version modified for the assault role (R3Y-2). The latter featured a raised flight deck to allow installation of an upward-opening bow door and landing ramps. In this form, loads such as six jeeps or two M3 half-tracks could be carried and disgorged directly onto a beach, as demonstrated here. In addition, both versions would have been able to provide support for the forward operation of seaplane fighters such as the Convair Sea Dart. In all, five R3Y-1s and six R3Y-2s were delivered, most of which joined VR-2 in 1956, but despite setting several time and distance records, they were plagued with engine problems, and after an accident in January 1958, the Tradewind was withdrawn from service. *NARA*

Following the cancellation of the carrier *United Sates* in 1949, the US Navy issued a specification for a jet-powered seaplane bomber in 1951 that would provide a viable alternative to the USAF's long-range B-52s. It was envisaged that a Seaplane Striking Force would operate from mobile bases and be capable of delivering both nuclear and conventional bombs. The result was the Glenn Martin P6M-1 SeaMaster, a swept-wing flying boat powered by four 10,000lb.s.t. (with afterburning) Allison J71-A-4 turbojets mounted above the wing. The prototype flew on 14 July 1955, but it, and the second prototype, were destroyed in crashes. Trials with production aircraft starting in 1958 revealed various issues which a re-engined and improved P6M-2 was expected to overcome. However, the whole programme was cancelled in 1959 and the Navy subsequently took on the nuclear strike role through the development of ballistic missile-carrying nuclear-powered submarines. *NARA*

Photo Credits

The following abbreviations at the end of each caption indicate the source and/or copyright of the relevant image.

AA/MD	Aviation Archive / McDonnell Aircraft Co.
ASM	Air Sea Media (author's copyright)
NARA	US National Archives and Records Administration (Still Image collection, College Park, Maryland)
NASA	National Aeronautics and Space Administration
NHHC	US Navy History and Heritage Command
NMNA	US Navy National Museum of Naval Aviation, Pensacola, Florida
USN	US Navy (non-attributed)

Bibliography

Chesnau, Roger, *Aircraft Carriers of the World: 1914 to the Present – An Illustrated Encyclopedia*, Arms & Armour Press, 1984.

Donald, David & March, Daniel J. (eds.), *Carrier Aviation: Air Power Directory*, Airtime Publishing, 2001.

Francillon, René J., *Tonkin Gulf Yacht Club*, Conway Maritime Press, 1988.

Friedman, Norman, *Carrier Air Power*, Conway Maritime Press, 1981.

Green, William, *War Planes of the Second World War: Fighters, Vol.4*, Macdonald & Co., 1961.

Hallion, Richard P., *The Naval Air War in Korea*, Nautical & Aviation Publishing Company of America, 1986.

Lenton, H.T., *American Battleships, Carriers and Cruisers*, Macdonald & Co., 1968.

Silverstone, Paul H., *US Warships since 1945*, Ian Allan, 1986.

Swanborough, Gordon & Bowers, Peter M., *United States Navy Aircraft since 1911*, second edition, 1976.

Terzibaschitsch, Stefan, *Aircraft Carriers of the US Navy*, Conway Maritime Press, 1980.

Thomas, Geoff, *US Navy Carrier Aircraft Colours*, Air Research Publications, 1989.

A selection of useful websites

aviationarchives.blogspot.com – A private website containing images and documentation covering US and other countries' military and civil aircraft.

www.seaforces.org – Contains detailed chronology on US aircraft carriers, their air wings and squadrons.

www.gonavy.jp – Details on the equipment and deployment of US Navy and USMC squadrons and air wings from 1943 to date.

www.history.navy.mil – Official website of the US Naval History and Heritage Command. Many digitised images online as well as access to numerous historic publications, accounts, and reports.

Amongst the mine of information available on Wikipedia is a page entitled US Navy and US Marine Corps aircraft tail codes, which was most useful in identifying the subjects of uncaptioned photographs.